How to Make Money from Blogging & Affiliate Marketing

A Guide on How to Create & Grow a WordPress Blog from Scratch with Google AdSense & Affiliate Marketing Monetization Secrets for Beginners

Lucrative Business Ideas Series
Book 2

Buzzer Joseph

Legal Disclaimer

The information contained in this book are business advice that for motivating young entrepreneurs. Most of them worked for the author. But there is no guarantee that it will yield the same result for you.

The author and publisher disclaim any liability arising directly or indirectly from the use of this book.

DEDICATION

This book is dedicated to God for giving me the inspiration to write this book for all young entrepreneurs, especially bloggers who wish to create a successful WordPress blog and monetize it through Google AdSense and Affiliate Marketing.

Table of Contents

INTRODUCTION

You cannot mention lucrative ways to earn passive income online without mentioning blogging. It is one of the long term online investments one can make and earn income on weekly or monthly basis.

Just like any other business, you don't just create a blog today and start making money immediately. It requires time, hard work and patience. You need to grow your blog and make it popular within or even beyond its niche. Once you have succeeded in creating and growing a blog, you can now start making money from it.

This book, *How to Make Money from Blogging & Affiliate Marketing* is written to guide you on how to create and build a blog from scratch and to also reveals the secrets on how to make money from your blog via Google AdSense, Affiliate Marketing and other Online Marketing strategies. I also revealed other lucrative ways to monetize your blog.

Here are some of the things you will learn in this book:

- **WordPress Blogging Guide:** Important Things to Consider in Order to Build a Successful Blog, How to Start a WordPress Blog the Right Way in 7 Easy Steps, How to Add a New Post in WordPress and Utilize all the Features, How to Install a WordPress Plugin – Step by Step for Beginners, Ways to Increase your Blog Traffic and Post Engagement for Free, Tips to Help You Build an Efficient Email Marketing Contact List, Best Free Small SEO Tools for Bloggers and How to Use them, How to Optimize your Blog Posts to Rank #1 on Search Engines, Best Sites to Buy Affordable SEO Optimized WordPress Themes, Best WordPress Blog and eCommerce Themes to Download, Best Cheap and Reliable Web Hosting Companies for Bloggers, Types of Blog Contents that Rank High and Drive Huge Traffic

- **Guest Blogging Guide:** How to Boost your Site Domain Authority with it, Things you should Check before Submitting Guest Post to any Site, Ways to Find Top Sites to Write Guest Posts for, How to Know the Authority Score of any Website, How to Discover the Best Guest Post Topic for any Site

- **Proven Ways to Make Money from your Blog:** Other Ways to Monetize your Blog Apart from AdSense & Affiliate Marketing

- **How to Make Money from Google AdSense:** 10 Simple Ways to Increase your Google AdSense Revenue by 105%

- **Complete Affiliate Marketing Guide:** Getting Started – Basic Thing you will Need for Successful Affiliate Marketing, Ways to Generate Traffic for your Affiliate Products, The Best Recommended Affiliate Programs, Things to Consider when Choosing an Affiliate Program, How to Find a Profitable Affiliate Marketing Niche, Different Ways to Make Money from Affiliate Marketing, Affiliate Marketing Tips and Tricks, Costly Mistakes that New Affiliate Marketers Make, The Various Forms of Affiliate Marketing Fraud

You will see a step by step guide to achieve all these, with pictures and screenshots to guide you. I also revealed all the mistakes I made when I started blogging newly and how I corrected them.

Now **explore this book** to create a long term passive income for yourself.

BLOGGING GUIDE: HOW TO START A SUCCESSFUL BLOG AND MAKE MONEY FROM IT

Blogging is one of the most lucrative online businesses you can start. Once you have successfully grown a blog, it keeps generating monthly income for you. It worth noting that it takes time and determination to succeed as a blogger. That is why many new blogger quit blogging after few months of creating a blog. You need a practical guide to help you do things right, so that you reap the fruit of your labour on the long run.

A blog (weblog) is simply a website where you update online readers or researchers with information on a particular category or group of categories (niche). A blog is a type of website where the content is presented in reverse chronological order (newer content appear first). Most company websites have blog sections where they update their subscribers on their company's plans and changes. It also helps new users searching for similar information on search engines to locate their websites and even patronize them.

I will reveal all you need in order to build a successful blog and the various ways you can monetize your blog.

Important Things to Consider in Order to Build a Successful Blog

It is very true that you can make a 6 figure, monthly income from blogging, but there are tips you need to know. You can only make money from a blog when it has become popular and successful. Blogging is a long term investment, it is never a "get-rich-quick" business. Once you have this in mind, then you will make money from your blog in due time.

Now let me reveal these important tips that will help you build a successful blog.

Here are some of the tips that will determine how successful your blog will be:

- Your blog niche/category

- The blogging platform

- Your blog domain name

- How user-friendly and search engine friendly it is

- The quality of the blog content and how search engine-friendly it is

- How well you promote your blog

Now let me explain these tips bit by bit.

Choosing the Right Blog Niche/Category

Before you even go ahead to setup a blog, you need to conclude on the category of information or articles you will be writing on your blog. There are 2 ways to choose a blog niche. You either choose a niche you have passion for, or choose a trending niche that is not yet saturated. I recommend the latter because a niche might be trending and also saturated. Example of such niche is tech, sports news, entertainment and celebrity news, tutorials, business, etc. Their search densities are high, but the competition is much that it might take a new blog up to a year of hard work to get noticed in that niche. Some trending niches that are not yet saturated are: **Fashion, Health and fitness, Online food recipes, Android games,** etc.

One of the secrets of breaking through in any blog niche is your ability to discover the information gap in that niche and then fill it up. This is why keyword research is very important.

You can combine more than one niche in your blog, but make sure the niches are related. For example, health and food recipes niches are related. But note that the more niches you add, the more works you have to do in order to get noticed in all those niches. Instead of combining multiple niches, you can concentrate on one and grow it faster.

Also, you can combine a trending seasonal niche with an evergreen niche that brings traffic all year round. For example, scholarship is a seasonal niche. You can combine it with tutorials on some trending software.

Discovering the best niche for your blog can be challenging at times. A smart way to go about this is to combine up to 3 different niches. With time, you shed off the unfavourable niches and concentrate on the favourable ones.

There are tons of blog categories or niches you can choose from. The infographics below reveals some popular broad blog categories.

Popular Blog Categories

Inventory of Specific Blog Categories in the Google Index
Taken May 16th, 2013 Using the Google "allintitle" Operator

Category	Count
Economics	130,000
Parenting	130,300
Career	190,600
Political	230,200
Finance	273,000
Pet	320,000
Gaming	322,000
Nature	390,000
DIY	395,000
Celebrity Gossip	420,000
Wine	452,000
Medical	465,000
Social Media	543,000
Cat	555,000
Sports	611,000
Entertainment	656,000
Shopping	712,000
Science	723,000
Education	741,000
Fitness	748,000
Business	762,000
Money	766,000
Dog	869,000
University	879,000
Lifestyle	896,000
Marketing	928,000
History	969,000
SEO	1,290,000
Technology	1,340,000
Green	1,510,000
Health	1,630,000
Law	1,780,000
Photography	1,800,000
Movie	1,830,000
Wedding	2,100,000
Food	2,190,000
Design	2,230,000
Travel	2,240,000
Beauty	2,260,000
Real Estate	2,370,000
Car	3,290,000
Fashion	3,380,000
Music	5,670,000

0 1 2 3 4 5 6

For more info visit http://www.wpromote.com/blog/seo/google-operators-infographic/

Popular blog categories

See: 10 Types of Blog Contents that Rank High and Drive Huge Traffic at
https://www.buzzingpoint.com/2019/09/high-ranking-blog-contents.html

Choosing a Blogging Platform

There are 2 popular blogging platforms: WordPress and Blogger (Google free blog platform). I recommend WordPress because you will have access to tons of free plugins that will help you grow and optimize your blogs faster. Also, you have total right over your blog. For a WordPress blog, you will need a hosting plan, a theme and a custom domain name. Before you decide to host your blog with a hosting company, first check the features available in the hosting plan you are opting for especially the band width. Go for a plan that offers high band width if you are planning to build a huge website with many media like movie, audio, etc.

Blogger.com is a free platform provided by Google to help bloggers who have the passion to build a blog but don't have money to start a paid hosting blog. One of the advantages of this platform is that you don't need to buy a hosting plan. Google hosts your blog for free. In order to use or create a blog on blogger, you must have an active gmail account. You can always create one for free at gmail.com. The con is that you must all Google blogger policies. Failure to do so might deny you access to your blog. Blogger offers a free ".blospot.com" domain name extension. But you can always buy and use a custom domain name which does not include the ".blogspot" extension.

Check out this **step by step guide on how to create and setup Blogger blog** at
http://www.microsofttut.com/2017/12/how-to-create-and-setup-new-blogger-blog.html.

What most new bloggers do is to start blogging on Google Blogger platform. Once they are ready to take blogging as a full time business, they switch the blog to WordPress. But I will advise you to start blogging on WordPress at once because if the Blogger-to-Wordpress switching is not properly done, you might lose your blog traffic and ranking.

If you wish to buy a hosting plan now, I recommend **BlueHost** because they are one of the most trusted web hosts in the world. There other recommended web hosts.

Check out the **7 Best Cheap and Reliable Web Hosting Companies for Bloggers** at
https://www.buzzingpoint.com/2020/04/best-blogging-web-hosts.html.

Choosing a Domain Name

Here comes another crucial aspect of blogging. Your domain name is a unique link that users will type in web browsers to be directed to your blog. Example, **www.YourDomainName.com**. Domain names are usually renewed annually. There are other available domain extensions apart from ".com" such as ".net", ".edu", ".org", ".info", etc.

These days, getting a good domain name is a difficult task. Here are tips to help you choose a good domain name that will help your blog grow faster:

- Don't choose a domain name that is too long. It might be a bit hard to remember, though there are long domain names that are easy to remember.

- Don't choose domain names that have many spelling options/alternatives. Someone else might buy the spelling alternative. Once your site visitors make a mistake in the spelling, they will land in your competitor's blog.

- Don't choose domain names that start with numbers.

- Look for a name that has one of your blog's keyword. For example, if you wish to blog on fashion, you check out a domain name like **Fashionwiki**, **Fashioncruise**, etc.

There are tons of domain registrars where you can purchase and register your blog domain name, but I recommend **BlueHost**. They are one of the most popular and most trusted domain registrars and web hosts in the world and also charge an affordable price.

Choosing a Good Blog Theme

The user-friendliness of your blog is determined to a large extent by your blog theme. A blog theme is a customizable framework of your blog.

A good WordPress theme has the following features:

- Ease of Customization
- Search engine optimized and user-friendly
- Affordable
- Premium support
- Updated regularly

See:

- **9 Best Sites to Buy Affordable SEO Optimized WordPress Themes** at https://www.buzzingpoint.com/2020/04/seo-friendly-wordpress-themes-sites.html.
- **7 Best WordPress Blog and eCommerce Themes to Download** at https://www.microsofttut.com/2020/04/wordpress-blog-ecommerce-themes.html

Always use premium themes because they offer advanced features that you will not enjoy in their free versions.

Writing Quality and Search Engine Optimized Blog Contents

Content has always been the king and will remain the king. That is why you need to go extra mile to write quality blog articles. It does not only end in writing quality blog articles, you also need to optimize them so that they will rank high on search engine result pages. Search Engine Optimization is simply the proper arrangement and usage of keywords so that search engines can properly crawl and index your web pages. Writing quality blog articles and proper SEO work hand in hand.

A quality blog article is always engaging. The idea flows smoothly and should never bore your blog readers. Your readers should always find your articles very interesting and also spend quality time there. An engaging blog post must not necessarily be too long. An article can be long without being useful or engaging. It can contain relevant links to other blog pages where some terms are explained better.

See:

- **How to Optimize your Blog Posts to Rank #1 on Search Engines** at https://www.buzzingpoint.com/2020/05/blog-seo-how-to-optimize-blog.html.
- **25 Best Free Small SEO Tools for Bloggers and How to Use them** at https://www.buzzingpoint.com/2020/03/best-small-seo-tools-bloggers.html.

Promoting your Blog

It does not end with creating a blog and writing quality blog articles. You need to go extra miles to promote your blog. There are many platforms and media where you can promote your blog and its articles both free and paid. Some of these platforms and media include: Facebook, Pinterest, Reddit, Quora, Mix, Email marketing, Google Ad, etc.

See:

- **15 Ways to Increase your Blog Traffic and Post Engagement for Free** at https://www.buzzingpoint.com/2020/05/how-to-increase-your-blog-traffic.html.
- **12 Tips to Help You Build an Efficient Email Marketing Contact List** at https://www.buzzingpoint.com/2020/04/build-email-marketing-contact-list.html.

Another effective way to promote your blog is by writing guest articles to popular blogs and online magazine sites. I will explain it elaborately in the next section of this book.

Check out the **Free Helpful Blogging Resources** section of this book's blogging guide to see how to achieve these important steps:

- How to Setup a WordPress Blog from Scratch
- How to Write a Post in WordPress
- How to Install and Activate a WordPress Plugin
- How to Secure a WordPress Blog

GUEST BLOGGING GUIDE: HOW TO BOOST YOUR SITE DOMAIN AUTHORITY WITH IT

Most Bloggers ask, "What is the easiest way to boost my blog Domain Authority?" For me, the answer is guest blogging. The benefits of guest blogging is numerous. But the most important ones is that it helps you drive quality traffic to your site and also helps your site become more popular.

Quality Backlink remains one of Google's top ranking factors. Not just getting a backlink from a top rated site. Google checks the relevance of the backlink page. So, if the content of the page you got the backlink does not have any relationship with the content of your site, the backlink will harm your site instead of boosting it. That is why you need to understand how guest posting works and the best way to do it.

Some other bloggers see it as waste of time to submit guest posts to other sites. They see no reason why they will spend hours, sometimes, even the whole day writing an article for another blog. But the truth is that the benefits worth the stress.

Before I go ahead to reveal the full benefits of guest blogging, let me properly explain it and how it works.

What is Guest Blogging?

Guest Blogging is the act of writing a well detailed article for another site, usually a top site in the same blogging niche with your site. In return, you get a backlink from the site, with your blog being mentioned there.

There are 2 types of backlinks: **do-follow** and **no-follow** backlinks.

Do-follow backlinks tell search engines that the landing page of the link is trusted and should be crawled and indexed. This means that if the landing page contains anything that goes against search engines policy, it might hurt both the domain of the landing page and the link source domain. That is why you need to be careful when requesting for do-follow backlink from any site.

No-follow backlinks tell search engine that the link's landing page is relevant, crawl it, but don't index it or use it to judge the domain of the link source. Most backlinks from post comments are no-follow backlinks.

So you now see that do-follow can boost your site authority if properly gotten and can also crash it if gotten the wrong way.

Benefits of Guest Blogging

Here are some of the benefits of submitting a quality guest post to a relevant top ranking site:

1. It is the best way to create awareness for a new brand or product.
2. Attracts more new blog readers who can become your regular audience, thereby helping to grow your traffic.
3. It is one of the ways to improve the SEO score of a website.
4. You can increase the authority of your company in the industry with guest posting.
5. It is the best way to boost your site Domain Authority (DA) and Page Authority (PA).

Things you should Check before Submitting Guest Post to any Site

Before you go ahead to submit a guest article to any site, there are some details about the site you should check to determine whether the do-follow backlink you will get from the site will benefit your site domain or not.

Use the Alexa Rank Tool

Alexa has a free ranking tool which is used to rank all the domains in the world, with the best site ranking number one.

First, check your site on Alexa rank tool by going to https://www.alexa.com/siteinfo.

Then enter your domain name in the search box. Click on **Run Analysis**.

Alexa domain name analysis

The tools run a quick analysis on your site reveals some other information about your site. It reveals the top keywords that bring traffic to the site, audience overlap, easy to rank keywords, audience geography, traffic source and total backlinks.

It also reveals the site's metrics like: **engagement** (the daily average page views per visitor), **daily time on site** (average time that a visitor spends on this site each day, in minutes and seconds), **bounce rate** (percentage of visitors that leave your site after one page view). A green colour near each of these metrics indicate a positive growth, while a red colour indicates a negative growth.

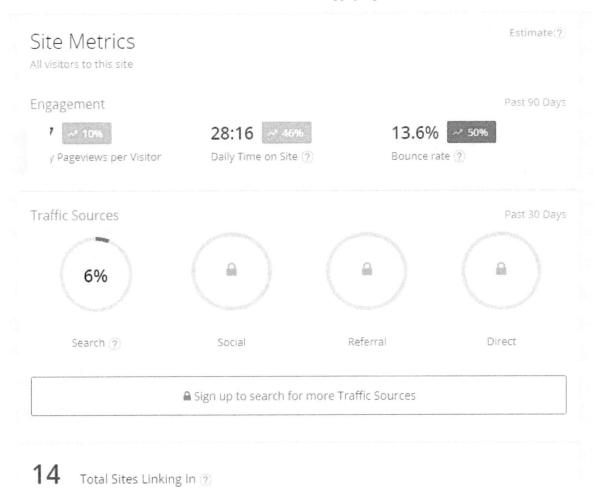

14 Total Sites Linking In ⑦

Domain analysis results

Take note of your top keywords, easy to rank keywords, audience geography, traffic source and all the site metrics (engagement, daily time, bounce rate).

Ways to Find Top Sites to Write Guest Posts for

Checking Alexa Similar Site by Audience Overlap

The easiest ways to find sites to write guest posts for is to check the sites that were displayed in the **Similar Sites by Audience Overlap** section of your site's Alexa rank analysis. Audience overlap score is calculated from an analysis of common visitors and/or search keywords. A site with a higher score shows higher audience overlap than a site with lower score.

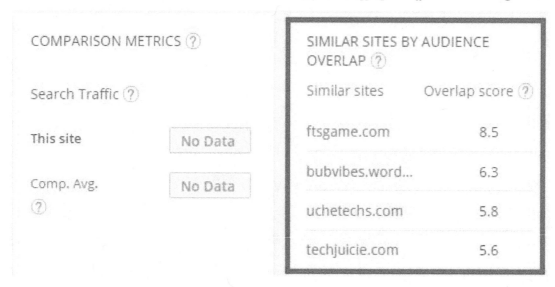

Similar sites by audience overlap

Not all these sites accept guest posts. You can check the site if they give you opportunity to write guest post for them. Some of them might have some other terms. Make sure you can meet all their guest post terms before writing to the site admin.

Use Google Search

Another easy way to find top sites that accept guest posts is to do a quick google search.

You can type, "**sites that accept guest posts**".

To make the result more specific, you can add the category of sites you want. For example, if your blog niche is business, you can search for "**business sites that accept guest post**".

You will see some blog posts with a list of guest post sites for different blog niches. Take time to gather as much as you can.

To ensure that the list of sites you have gathered is accurate, check out the suggested sites on your list one after the other. Some sites stop accepting guest posts after a certain period of time. So make sure they still accept guest posts.

How to Know the Authority Score of any Website

Now that you have gathered a list of sites in your blogging niche, you need to check their domain authority, page authority and moz rank scores. This is because the higher the score of any site you wish to submit a guest post for, the higher the positive impact it will have on your blog domain.

Domain authority and page authority were proposed by SEOMoz to calculate the authority of any domain in a scale of hundred.

There are many free online tools you can use to check these scores, but a popular one I use and recommend is https://websiteseochecker.com/domain-authority-checker/.

Visit the tool site. Now open your site list and copy the first 3 domain names and paste them on the search box. Check the reCAPTCHA box to verify that you are not a robot. Then click on **Check**.

Domain Authority Checker - DA checker - Check domain authority

Buy Relevant DA 40+, PA40+ Backlinks from 3$ Now

Check DA

The tool will analyze all the sites you have pasted their domain URL and display the results in about 18 columns including the Alexa rank.

There are few columns you should neglect. Pay attention to these columns:

- **DA** (Domain Authority)
- **PA** (Page Authority)
- **TB** (Moz Trust Backlinks)
- **QB** (Moz Quality Backlinks)
- **PQ** (Percentage of Quality Backlinks)
- **MT** (Moz Trust)
- **SS** (Moz Spam Score) - The higher the spam score, the worst the backlink profile.
- **TC** (Traffic Country) - Important if you want to target traffic from a particular geo location.
- **IX** (Number of Indexed URLS) - The higher the number, the more authoritative the domain.
- **DF** (DoFollow backlinks)

URL	DA	PA	TB	QB	PQ	MT	SS	OS	Age	Alexa	TC	TF	CF	IX	DF	BL	DH
Website Authority - Check all URLs on single click - Sign up																	
www.namasteui..	30	39	27K	42	0%	4	1%	42%	4Y, 309D	147,354		13	42	52K	59%	🔗	🕐
www.dzone.com	81	64	82K	56K	68%	6	1%	74%	21Y, 364D	3,850		28	40	2M	76%	🔗	🕐
www.dev.to	75	47	281	218	78%	5	22%	66%		8,661		29	32	43	97%	🔗	🕐

Website authority results

Now compare the result of each site and pick out the ones that their DA is below 25. Repeat this for all the domain names in your list and eliminate the poor ranking sites.

Next, you need to run the same Alexa rank analysis for these sites that passed the authority test. Also note all the metrics I mentioned earlier, especially the engagement and bounce rate.

Now compare the results of the site and those of your site. Check their top keywords and also the traffic sources and site flow.

Choose the ones whose top keywords are related to your site's top keywords.

Eliminate the sites that have low organic traffic, unrelated keywords and very poor engagement and high bounce rate.

By now, your list will contain very few number of sites. It is now time to find what post categories perform best for each site.

How to Discover the Best Guest Post Topic for any Site

Before now, you have a list of topics you want to write on as guest posts. Compare these topics and make some of the keywords of these topics are related to those top keywords Alexa suggested when you ran analysis for these guest post sites.

For example, if one of your proposed topics is "**How to make money from a blog**". Check for the site that has make money as one of its top keywords.

Now go to the site and search for that topic to ensure it has not been written. Do not use the whole title phrase. Pick some keywords like "**make money blog**". If the topic has not been covered, then you are free to write on it.

To make sure your guest post properly suits the site's audience, check their popular posts and make sure the topic is related to those that are popular on the site.

Some Tips to Make your Guest Article more Acceptable

Many top sites have a circle of other site owners they love to work with. These are sites they interact with often. Some are their great fans who read their posts regularly.

In order to ensure your guest post is not turned down, consider following the site closely, check some of their recent posts and drop meaningful comments. You might consider introducing yourself at the last paragraph of your comment. Do it about 3 to 5 times before contact the blog. You might also consider sharing some of their posts on twitter. Include the blog owner's twitter username when sharing the posts. This will help you get a feedback faster when you pitch your guest post.

Also make sure you follow the site's guest post guidelines. They have some specifications. Make sure your article content met all their criteria.

Now when writing the guest post email, address the blog owner by his or her name. Don't use **Dear Sir** or **Dear Ma**. Most site owners hate this. Even me in particular.

Introduce yourself and mention your blog name. Give your reasons why you want to guest blog on their sites. You can showcase your blogging potential by giving a link to one or two of your guest articles that have been published elsewhere.

A good guest article is the one which the guest site visitors will find it difficult to know that it was not written by the site owner or the site editors. Follow their writing and formatting styles.

Another way to make the site owner easily approve your article is to include some of their related posts as inbound links in your guest article. This is one of the best ways to prove that you are one of their great fans and a proficient writer. Just one or two keywords from the article's title and search it on their site. You will see some related articles that have been published on the site. Add their links where appropriate.

To improve your guest article's engagement, encourage their blog readers to comment by adding a call to action at the end of your article.

Most sites don't allow guest bloggers to include their site links within the guest article (they are mostly indicated in the guest post guidelines). That is why you need to craft a very engaging Author bio, where you talk about yourself and probably advertise your brand. You have a target for writing a guest article. It could be to boost your site traffic, get more social media followers or even grow your email subscriber list. Whichever it is, the author bio is the right place to add the link. But make sure you don't add more than one in this section.

How to Make Sure your Guest Article Converts

It does not just end in writing a guest post and getting your content approved. You need to ensure that many readers see your guest post on daily basis by sharing the post link on your own social media platforms and even sending a notification to your email subscribers about the article and the link.

Also, don't just write one guest post and relax. Keep discovering new top sites that accept guest posts in your niche. You can also submit more than one guest article to a particular site as long as you are meeting your target and the site owner is willing to accept more guest articles from you.

Conclusion

There you are! You have seen the best way to go about guest blogging, its benefits, how to find the most suiting guest blogging site and how to write an engaging guest article that will convert well and be far from rejection. Now the ball is in your court.

Let's now go over to the most interesting part of blogging – **ways to make money with your blog**.

DIFFERENT WAYS TO MAKE MONEY FROM YOUR BLOG

The most exciting aspect of blogging is making money from your blog. After the hard work and stress of writing great blog articles and promoting your blog, you need to make monetize your blog and the most out of it.

There are many ways to make money from your blog. Though you might not be utilizing all of them at the same time, you can combine one or two of them. Some of the popular ways to make money from your blog include:

- Google AdSense and Other Paid Ad Networks
- Affiliate Marketing

Other Proven Ways to Monetize a Blog

Apart from affiliate marketing and joining ad networks, there are other ways to monetize your blog. But always know that you can only make money from your blog when you have grown and promoted it. Here are some of the lucrative ways to make money from a blog.

- Offer a Paid Membership Plan on your Blog
- Accept Donations on your Blog (if your blog is a non-profit blog)
- Sell Physical Products Online Using WordPress
- Accept Sponsored Articles on your Blog
- Become a Freelance Blogger in your Niche
- Sell Digital Products like EBooks to your Blog Audience
- Create and Sell Online Courses
- Start a Coaching/Consulting Business

Check out: 30 Proven Ways to Make Money Online Blogging with WordPress at
https://www.wpbeginner.com/beginners-guide/make-money-online/

You will learn how to make money from Google AdSense and Affiliate Marketing in the next 2 sections.

HOW TO MAKE MONEY FROM GOOGLE ADSENSE

Google AdSense is one of the avenues to monetize your blog. If you have grown your blog and now getting up to 50% of your traffic from search engines, you can apply for Google AdSense – a Pay per Click ad network program introduced by Google. Once your site is approved, ads will start displaying. Once your site visitors click on the ads, you earn money. Google AdSense is the largest and most popular monetization program for publishers. Unlike other monetization programs, Google AdSense does not strictly base more on number of traffic you get on your blog, rather they base on quality of the traffic sources.

Are you ready to apply for Google AdSense? Make sure your blog meets the basic requirements.

I shared these requirements and how to ensure your blog meets them in this article: **How to Optimize your Blog and Videos for Fast Google AdSense Approval** at https://www.buzzingpoint.com/2020/05/how-to-get-google-adsense-approval.html.

How to Apply for Google AdSense

1. Login to the Gmail account you wish to use for the AdSense application. Make sure the email account is not associated with any AdSense account.

2. Open a new tab and go to https://www.google.com/adsense. Click on **Get Started** as shown below.

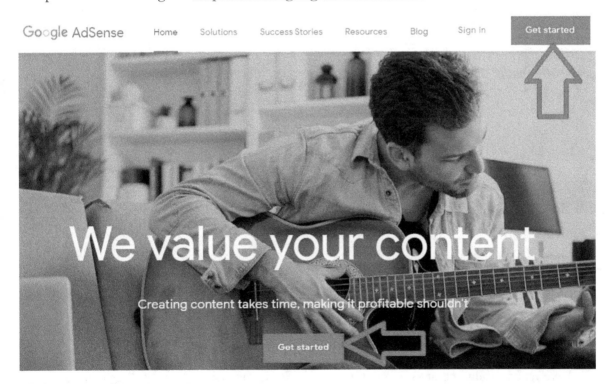

Click on get started

3. Now follow the screen to screen guide to sign up for Google AdSense. You will be required to enter your domain name, email address. Specify that you wish to be notified on customized help and performance suggestions. Then click on **Save and Continue** as shown below.

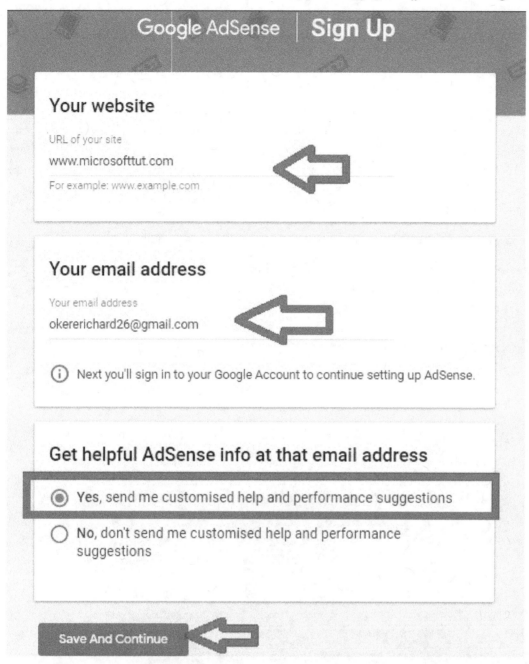

Enter your domain name and email address

4. Next is to sign into your Google account.

5. Now specify your country or territory. Always select your own country so that you will be able to provide the AdSense account verification requirements.

6. Review and accept the AdSense Terms and Conditions. Next, click on Create account.

7. **Congrats!** You have successfully created your Google AdSense account. Now follow the guide at https://support.google.com/adsense/answer/7402256 to **connect your site** and **enter your payment details**. For some countries, you might be required to verify your phone number.

NOTE: To add AdSense verification code to your site you will need a plugin. Use this plugin - **Insert Headers and Footers** by WPBeginner. The plugin helps you to insert code or text in the header or footer of your WordPress blog.

Google AdSense Recommended Alternatives

Google AdSense is not the only recommended ad network for monetizing your blog. In fact Google AdSense is not the highest paying ad network. There are other recommended ad networks for bloggers. But most of them require that your blog to meet a particular range of page view monthly. Some of these recommended alternatives to Google AdSense include:

- Media.net
- Adversal
- Taboola Native Advertising
- Infolinks
- Propeller Ads
- Revcontent Native Advertising
- Adsterra
- MGID

Feel free to check up these ad networks and their requirements and policies. They are also compatible with Google AdSense. So you can combine one of them with Google AdSense on your blog if you wish.

Now that you have successfully got a Google AdSense, the next challenge might be how to increase your earnings. I shared some secrets and tips below.

10 Simple Ways to Increase your Google AdSense Revenue by 105%

After your site got approved of Google AdSense, the next big question is, How to boost your daily earnings. These days, Google AdSense has tightened their belt and will not tolerate any form of illegal act or shortcut. If you are ready to play by Google AdSense rules and provide quality contents and traffic, they will reward. Not only these, these are few tweaks that can make your daily revenue from AdSense to double up.

Initially I thought that I could make more money by add more ad units to my blog posts. But I got a negative result. I also tried generating traffic through illegal source, my AdSense account was nearly blocked. I faced **limited ad serving** issue because of it. That was what made me look for the right way to do things and boost my earnings.

I have ran multiple experiments with Google AdSense ad placement and have discovered few tips that made a difference in terms of revenue. I tried these results on my other sites and they also yielded positive returns. I will reveal these AdSense revenue-boosting tips that will also help you if you implement them.

Do Not Violate any Google AdSense Policy

This is the first thing you should bear in mind. Check if your site and its contents are violating any Google AdSense Policy at https://support.google.com/adsense/answer/48182. Make sure you don't use any illegal means to generate traffic to your blog. Never by any means deceive your readers to click on your ads. Don't publish any content that promotes immorality like pornography, homosexuality, lesbianism, betting, etc. Don't add Google ad codes on pages that have little or no value, like your **Contact us**, **About Us**, Privacy **Policy pages**, etc.

Google AdSense will give you the best if you keep to their policies.

Write Quality Blog Articles

Right from the time you were applying for google AdSense, you know strict Google has been when it comes to checking the quality of a blog content. It does not end after Google AdSense application. Don't relax because you have got a fully approved AdSense account. In fact, this is now the right time to double your effort with regards to writing quality contents.

Quality content does not mean a very lengthy blog post without any value. Always carry out proper keyword research before you start writing. Know what readers are looking for and over deliver with your blog posts. Make your blog posts detailed so that it can engage your readers. The more time a user spends on your blog, the more ads will convert if they eventually click one.

The more value your blog has, the more quality ads Google will channel to your Ad units.

Get more of your Daily Blog Traffic from Search Engines

Google loves organic traffic from search engines. Quality ads are served to sites that get more of their daily traffic from search engines and a few percentage from other legal sources. Audience directed to your site by search engines spend more time on your blog than those that came from social media. This is because people search for information they need on search engines. So when search engines recommends your site by ranking it top on search results, they will take time to read your blog content to make sure they get all the solutions they have been looking for.

Writing the best article does not mean you will rank in the first page when people search for the information. You need to also optimize your blogs for search engines, properly use relevant keywords so that they will properly crawl your blog pages and rank it high.

Ensure that your Blog Gets Enough Traffic

Even though AdSense does not lay much emphasis on the number of daily blog traffic in their policy, you can earn more by just getting more daily traffic. Always target more than one thousand daily page views if you want earn more from your blog.

Even if you placed only one ad unit and got few clicks, those few clicks will convert more if you have much page views. Once you cross one thousand unique page views and your site has generated more than 1000 impressions that day, you will earn whatever is displayed in your AdSense account's RPM. This is the revenue per thousand impression.

Google calculates your RPM by dividing your estimated earnings by the number of page views and them multiplying it by 1000.

So let's assume your current page view at a particular time of a day is 500 and your estimated earning is $10, then your RPM will be:

(10/500)*1000 = $20

The more page views you get, the higher your earnings.

Target Traffics from US and UK

Traffic from locations like US and UK helps to increase your CPC. So the more traffic you get from these locations, the more clicks users from these locations will give you.

You can boost your traffic from these locations by running targeted paid traffic campaign on Facebook ads or Google ads. But remember to remove all Google AdSense codes from your site until you are through with the paid campaign.

It is against Google AdSense policy to run paid traffic campaign while Google ads are being displayed on your site. They feel that your main intention is to increase the number of clicks and earnings. So, to avoid facing any ban or suspension, remove the code until you are through with the paid traffic campaign.

Make Sure your Site Theme is Responsive if you are Using Responsive Ad Units

It is against Google Policy to use a responsive ad unit on a non-responsive site. A responsive site is one that automatically adjusts itself to different view ports; mobile, iPad, PC, etc.

If your site theme is not responsive then use a non-responsive ad unit. But why must you use a non-responsive theme or a theme that is not mobile friendly? It does not have any advantage. Users will not spend more time on any blog that is not responsive.

More than 70% of total internet activities are done with mobile devices. So you need to give these category that gives a higher percentage daily traffic a higher priority.

Download and use mobile-friendly and SEO optimized themes so that search engines will like your site.

Use Responsive Ad Units throughout

Whether you are creating a link, text or image ad unit, always go with the responsive option. Responsive ad units are more competitive than those that are not responsive. This is because it can display any size of ad, unlike non-responsive ad units where the dimension of the ad has been defined.

Add Fewer Ad Units

One mistake most bloggers make is adding many ad units in their blog posts, thinking that it will yield more revenue. No, it does not. Instead, it reduces your potential revenue by giving room for low quality ads to show.

But if you reduce the number of ad units, your ad units become more competitive. This means that ads that have more value will be displayed. The more ad units waste, the more your CPC drops.

I have personally experimented this on my blog. I once added 5 ad units to my blog and took note of the revenue for one week. Then I later reduced the ad units to 3. I noticed that my earnings almost doubled.

Place your Ad Units at the Right Locations

The location of your ad units on your blog pages matters a lot. You need to place them right so that they will perform better. Place most of your ad units within your blog post content because this is where your blog audience pay more attentions.

Ads within blog post contents perform better and even attract more clicks than those place beside the header or in the side bar. Place an ad unit after your post's first paragraph. So that readers will see it immediately after reading the first paragraph.

Do Not Add more than One Ad Unit in your Side Bar

Like I said earlier, add few ad units ensures that only quality ads are displayed. It also helps to reduce the redundancy of ads, thus giving ads that have higher CPC to display in your ad units. One of the easiest ways to ensure that ads do not in waste is to add most of your ad units within your blog post content and adding one in the side bar.

Remember that most page views come from mobile device. Also in the mobile view of your blog theme, the side bar appears below the post content. Most users don't go beyond the blog content. So fewer audience will even see side ads.

Use Auto Ads if you have Long Article Contents

Google introduced auto ads so that they can help you place ads in locations where they will perform best. Auto ads will display different ad formats like:

- **In-page Ads:** Ads that appear within the main body of content on your pages.
- **Matched Content:** Content promotion tool that can increase revenue and engagement.
- **Anchor Ads:** Ads that stick to the edge of the user's screen and are easily dismissible.
- **Vignette Ads:** Mobile full-screen ads that appear between page loads.

You only add one code to your site header, then Google takes care of the rest.

The easiest plugin for adding the auto ad code to your site's header is the **Insert Headers and Footers** plugin. If you do not want to use auto ads, you can insert ad unit code at any spot in your blog with the **Insert Post Ads** plugin. Once you turn ON auto ad and add the code to your site, ads will show at relevant locations as determined by Google.

To turn ON auto ads, login to your AdSense account admin dashboard. Navigate to **Ads >> Overview**. In the **By Site** tab, scroll down and click on the **Edit** icon as shown below.

How to turn on auto ads

You will be taken to the auto ad **Site Settings**. Now turn on auto ads by shifting the slider to the right. Also turn on the **Optimize your existing ad units** button. Save your setting by clicking on **Apply to Site**.

How to Make Money from Blogging & Affiliate Marketing

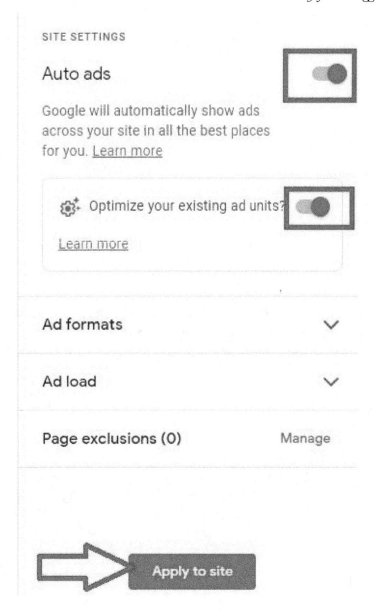

Activate auto ads

Auto ads work well and can yield a higher revenue if you optimize it properly. At the default setting, it will add many ad units to your blog posts, which may end up reducing your CPC.

The best way to get the best from auto ad is to turn off other ad formats except **In-page Ads**. Also set the **Ad Control** to show the minimum number of ads as shown below. Don't forget to save your current settings by clicking on **Apply to Site**.

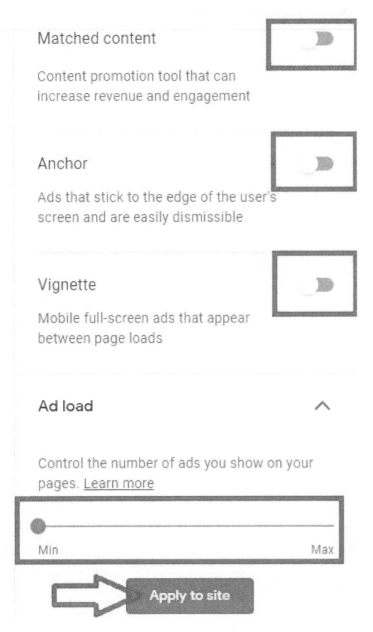

Ad load cotrol

You will see the estimated number of ads that will appear in your blog pages in the Preview section.

You can also use auto ads together with some custom ad units. In my blog pages, I used a heat map to detect the spot where audience more attention to. It happens to be around the third paragraph. So to make the very best use of this spot, I created a responsive ad unit and inserted it after the third paragraph. You can do the same for your site.

Do Not Use Link Ads if you have Huge Daily Traffic

Make out time and check top site who use AdSense. You will notice that they don't use Link ads. Link ads attract more ad clicks, but reduce your page engagement, especially when placed in the first or second paragraph. And the funny thing about link ads is that they attract more clicks but don't yield much revenue.

I once carried out an experiment with link ads on my site. When I added it to my my site, I got an average of 70 daily ad clicks, but my earning was still poor. So after a week, I removed it and replaced it with a responsive ad unit. The ad clicks reduced, but my earnings doubled up. I also noticed that my CPC also increased.

If you have up to 1000 daily page views on your blog, don't bother using link ads. Rather use few responsive image/text ads. You will see a very big positive difference in your earnings.

Conclusion

Increasing your AdSense is gradual process that requires constant experiment. It took me up to 3 months to discover the best settings that yields the best results for my blog. I always experiment any new idea for one week and then take note of the result. After running experiment, I analyze the results and compare it with the result of my previous findings. These are some of the tips that have really helped me boost my AdSense earnings. I tested them in my 2 blogs and the result was very similar.

Feel free to try them on your site. Run experiment with responsive image/text ad units and link ads units and know what best works for you. You may try combining both types, but don't put link ad units in the first or second paragraphs. They will reduce your site's reader's engagement and still yield less revenue. Tell me the combination that works for you.

FREE HELPFUL BLOGGING RESOURCES

How to Start a WordPress Blog the Right Way in 7 Easy Steps - https://www.wpbeginner.com/start-a-wordpress-blog/

How to Add a New Post in WordPress and Utilize all the Features - https://www.wpbeginner.com/beginners-guide/how-to-add-a-new-post-in-wordpress-and-utilize-all-the-features/

How to Install a WordPress Plugin – Step by Step for Beginners - https://www.wpbeginner.com/beginners-guide/step-by-step-guide-to-install-a-wordpress-plugin-for-beginners/

The Ultimate WordPress Security Guide – Step by Step - https://www.wpbeginner.com/wordpress-security/

10 Types of Blog Contents that Rank High and Drive Huge Traffic - https://www.buzzingpoint.com/2019/09/high-ranking-blog-contents.html

15 Ways to Increase your Blog Traffic and Post Engagement for Free - https://www.buzzingpoint.com/2020/05/how-to-increase-your-blog-traffic.html

YouTube SEO: How to Optimize your YouTube Videos for Better Ranking - https://www.buzzingpoint.com/2020/05/how-to-optimize-youtube-videos.html

Blog SEO: How to Optimize your Posts to Rank #1 on Search Engines - https://www.buzzingpoint.com/2020/05/blog-seo-how-to-optimize-blog.html

15 Essential Free WordPress Plugins for Top Security and SEO - https://www.buzzingpoint.com/2020/04/wordpress-plugins-security-seo.html

9 Best Sites to Buy Affordable SEO Optimized WordPress Themes - https://www.buzzingpoint.com/2020/04/seo-friendly-wordpress-themes-sites.html

7 Best Cheap and Reliable Web Hosting Companies for Bloggers - https://www.buzzingpoint.com/2020/04/best-blogging-web-hosts.html

7 Best WordPress Blog and eCommerce Themes to Download - https://www.microsofttut.com/2020/04/wordpress-blog-ecommerce-themes.html

How to Optimize your Blog and Videos for Fast Google AdSense Approval - https://www.buzzingpoint.com/2020/05/how-to-get-google-adsense-approval.html

9 Secrets To Getting An Approved Google Adsense & Why Your Applications Were Rejected - https://www.microsofttut.com/2017/08/9-secrets-to-getting-approved-google-adsense.html

7 Simple Strategies To Increase Your Google Adsense Earnings - https://www.microsofttut.com/2017/08/7-simple-strategies-to-increase-your-adsense-earning.html

12 Tips to Help You Build an Efficient Email Marketing Contact List - https://www.buzzingpoint.com/2020/04/build-email-marketing-contact-list.html

How To Submit Website & Sitemap To Google & Bing Search Engines - https://www.microsofttut.com/2017/10/how-to-submit-your-sitemaps-to-google-and-bing.html

Review Of BlueHost - One Of The Most Recommended Web Hosting Companies - https://www.microsofttut.com/2018/05/bluehost-recommended-web-hosting-company.html

How To Set Up Your Custom Email To Send And Receive Emails Through Gmail - https://www.microsofttut.com/2018/05/how-to-set-up-your-custom-email-to-send-and-receive-mail-through-gmail.html

15 Simple Ways To Increase Your Website Traffic For Free - https://www.microsofttut.com/2018/01/free-simple-ways-to-increase-your-website.html

7 Things to Consider In Order to Build A Successful Blog/Website - https://www.microsofttut.com/2017/12/things-to-consider-for-a-successful-blog.html

10 Best, Free And Paid SEO Tools To Boost Your Site SEO Ranking - https://www.microsofttut.com/2018/01/10-best-free-and-paid-tools-to-boost-your-site-seo.html

How To Boost Your Site SEO With Google Tag Manager - https://www.microsofttut.com/2017/10/how-boost-your-site-seo-with-google-tag.html

COMPLETE AFFILIATE MARKETING GUIDE

Apart from ad networks, another good way to monetize your blog is through affiliate marketing, an aspect of digital marketing. Although affiliate marketing can be done without having a blog. But having a blog gives you more advantage. Search engines will help you locate real buyers, even while you sleep. So you make more money.

What is Affiliate Marketing?

Affiliate marketing is a marketing model designed so that individuals can help companies sell more of their products and services both online and offline. As an affiliate marketer (also known as publisher), you will work within a referral based system that allows you to earn a cut of the money that companies make from sales made to people that you refer.

Affiliate marketing is the arrangement whereby an affiliate earns a commission for completing an agreed-upon marketing objective. Commonly, the affiliate markets products and services belonging to a third party, and they earn a commission for each customer they bring on board.

This economic arrangement has existed for as long as businesses have been around, but it became much more pronounced in the age of the internet. There are many affiliate marketers who earn six and seven figures. The beauty of affiliate marketing is that there are almost no barriers, and all you need is an internet connection, and you are good to go.

Most people who are stuck in a boring corporate job and would like to escape the rat race would do really well by crossing over to the world of affiliate marketing. As an affiliate marketer, you could even choose to work from the comfort of your home, and your earning potential will be governed by your depth of hunger for success.

There's considerable work to be done, especially in the early stages, and then you can put up systems that will make your work all the easier. Also, the world of affiliate marketing is ever-changing, and an affiliate marketer must keep reinventing themselves so that they don't lose to their competition.

Advertising is a common theme in the world of affiliate marketing. Besides picking a profitable product, your advertising methods will play a critical role in determining your overall success. Some of the popular advertising methods include display advertisement, social media advertisement, email marketing, video advertisement, and blogging.

Most businesses have embraced affiliate marketers, as that's one of the best ways to increase business revenue and brand visibility. As an affiliate marketer, there are key things you must pay attention to, or else you are at risk of sabotaging your efforts. The two main things you must carefully select are the product and the merchants. Working with transparent merchants ensures that your hard work doesn't go down the drain.

Affiliate marketing is one of the best ways to escape the rat race, create time for the things (and people) you care about, and, most importantly, attain financial freedom.

In summary, here are the steps involved in affiliate marketing:

- You partner with a company to help them promote a product or service.
- You market and send traffic to these products using your own resources.
- Some of those people purchase the product based on your recommendation.
- You get paid a commission for those purchases. Simple!

How Much Can You Make With Affiliate Marketing?

The amount of money that you can earn with affiliate marketing will depend on the product that you choose to promote. Often times, this amount can be up to 100% of the total price of the product.

The hungrier you are, the more work you put in, and thus the more money that flows to your side, but if you are lazy, then expect to make little money and in some cases, no money at all. Just because affiliate marketing offers freedom doesn't mean that money will automatically flow into your bank account.

You can promote both high and low ticket products as an affiliate. Low ticket products range in price from $1 to $99 and high ticket from $100 upwards. Generally, affiliate marketers classify low cost products as low-ticket affiliate products and those that are more expensive to be high-ticket affiliate products. As you start in the affiliate marketing business, you need to decide whether you want to promote cheap or expensive items. Most affiliate marketers choose to promote low-ticket affiliate products because they think that it is easier to convince people to buy cheap items. However, this also means that you need to sell more items to earn more money.

Benefits of affiliate marketing

There has never been a better time to start an affiliate marketing business than today, and the opportunity continues to grow every day as millions of people turn to the internet to purchase new products and services. In the next 10 years, more than 80% of all business transactions will be through the internet.

Experienced marketers know this, and they know that affiliate marketing is not going anywhere anytime soon. Therefore, if you want to make money online, it is very important that you take this information seriously and follow these instructions as close as possible so that you also take your cut from this pie.

Here are a few more reasons to start an affiliate marketing business today:

Very Easy to Get Started

Affiliate marketing is one of the best and easiest ways for anyone to make money online. It is a billion dollar a year industry with a very low barrier of entry. You don't need any special degrees or high technical knowledge to make it work. The door is pretty much open to anyone willing to step inside.

You can Start with Very Little or No Investment

Affiliate marketing does not require a big initial investment. If you are strapped on cash, there are plenty of free strategies that you can use in order to find people on the internet who are interested in buying whatever you promote.

You can Make Money Selling Products that Fall within your Passion

Another lovely aspect of affiliate marketing is that you can earn good money while promoting products or services within your passion. Amazon.com alone has one of the biggest affiliate programs, and if you have ever shopped on their site, you can attest that they pretty much sell everything. So you can earn commissions promoting whatever items fall within your passion, without getting bored.

You can Work from the Comfort of your Room

All you need is a computer and an internet connection. Also, you work at your own convenience. All you need is to plan your working hours.

Who is Affiliate Marketing for?

Affiliate marketing is for people willing to create a new source of income through the internet. When done right, affiliate marketing is an excellent way to make cool money online. If you dedicate your time enough to master the affiliate marketing game, you can earn incredible amounts of money right from the comfort of your home, as long as you have a computer and an internet connection at hand.

Getting Started – Basic Things you will Need for Successful Affiliate Marketing

Here are the things you will need to start affiliate marketing business:

A Website

Most affiliate programs require that you have a website before you will be accepted. Advertisers check the website to see what types of content you have. Some advertisers are extremely picky when choosing affiliates. They only accept those whose websites can bring in huge amounts of traffic. Don't worry though, because there are also beginner level affiliate marketing programs that will accept even publishers with new websites.

A Profitable Niche

You cannot just create any type of website if you want to become a successful affiliate marketer. In particular, you need to be careful in choosing the niche market. Always remember that the types of affiliate marketing products that you can sell will depend on the niche market you choose to participate in.

If you want to sell only high ticket items for instance, you need to make sure that the niche market you have chosen have high-ticket affiliate marketing programs.

An Organic Source of Traffic

As far as internet marketing is concerned, there are two ways for you to get traffic, **organic** and **paid**. While some affiliate marketers do use paid methods to earn through affiliate marketing, these methods expose you to a higher financial risk. Those who use these methods have developed their skill over years of trial and error.

For now, you should focus on building assets that will help you gather organic visitors. This includes social media accounts and pages, forum memberships, accounts in niche specific online communities, offline traffic sources and other similar assets. You will need to think about where you will get your traffic for your website if you want to be successful from day one.

A Membership to an Affiliate Marketing Program

There are tons of affiliate marketing programs in the web. However, not all of them will be suitable to offer to the type of traffic that you can get. You will need to choose an affiliate program that fits the needs of the audience. We will discuss how to choose the best affiliate marketing programs for your audience in the following chapters. The four factors above are the minimum requirements for becoming a successful affiliate marketer.

After choosing an affiliate marketing program, you can apply directly from the web. Most of the application processes just require you to fill up a form with your personal details. In addition, the application form may also ask how you plan to generate traffic for your affiliate offers and what types of products you wish to promote.

The form may also ask you how much traffic your own website gets a day and what other monetization methods you use in the said website.

In addition, you may be asked to fill up a tax form. This part will depend on the requirements of the country of origin of the affiliate program. When signing up for Amazon Associates for Amazon.com for instance, US citizens will be asked to fill up a US tax form. A different form will be required if you are applying for Amazon.ca (Canada) Associates program.

How Hard is the Application Process?

For some affiliate programs, getting in is easy. Some may even automatically approve your application. There are more specialized programs though, that will ask for more requirements after you apply. The most demanding programs will have their employees scan your website for the quality of the content. If they are not satisfied with the design or the quality of the content of your website, they may reject your application. These extremely selective programs usually do this for different reasons.

The majority of them do it because they want to protect their brand. Big brands only want to be associated with websites that have good quality content. Some of them will only accept websites that have been around for a long time with hundreds of archived content. Some brands will also reject your application if they see that your website or your contents are not aligned with their target consumers. If your website is in English, for example and your and you apply with an affiliate program for Spanish people, you are likely to be rejected.

How Do You Get Paid as an Affiliate Marketers?

Considering there are diverse products and services being promoted, there are bound to be diverse metrics of paying the affiliate marketers. What is important is for the affiliate marketer to understand what's asked of them and align themselves with the program that promises the greatest rewards. For instance, if you run a real estate website, it would make more financial sense to sign up to an affiliate program that seeks emails belonging to potential real estate customers as opposed to signing up for an affiliate program that seeks web-hosting customers.

The following are the common metrics upon which an affiliate marketer is compensated.

Pay per sale: In this case, an affiliate marketer receives a commission for every person they get to purchase a product. Affiliate networks are chock full of brands that are looking to grow their sales volume. If you have an established blog, you have a head start, and you may recommend products that are aligned to your audience, and you will see your commissions accumulating. You may also engage in media buying and target your traffic so that they will convert into customers. Ensure that you are slow and deliberate as opposed to being unpractical. Careless mistakes can cost you a fortune.

Pay per click: Not every merchant is merely looking to make a sale. There are some merchants who are looking to expand their visibility. And they are ready to pay an affiliate marketer to bring targeted audience to their website. Thus, for every click you send to their website, the merchant happily pays you a commission.

For some reason, affiliate marketers, especially newbies, might feel the need to take advantage of the situation and send illegitimate clicks so they may inflate their commissions, which almost always ends badly for them. Ensure that you are transparent in your efforts to earn a commission. As an affiliate marketer, you only succeed when the merchant/brand succeeds, and if you are a fraud, you are contributing to the brand's demise, and should you be successful, that's one less employer off the market. It never ends well.

Pay per lead: data is one of the most valuable elements of successful businesses, and merchants and firms are well aware of this fact. They are willing to pay affiliate marketers to collect data on their target clients. The most valuable datum is the email address. There are many affiliate programs that compensate marketers for every email belonging to a target audience that they bring aboard. Most merchants and affiliate networks pay out commissions weekly and monthly.

There might be restrictions on newbies, but once they earn a considerable amount, the restrictions are lifted. Depending on your location and the affiliate network or merchant in question, there are many ways that the affiliate marketer receives their commissions, including bank transfers, checks, and e-payment platforms like PayPal and Paxum.

How Does Affiliate Marketing Work?

In order to understand how affiliate marketing works, you first have to become aware of the key players. The more understanding you have about these key players, the more your capacity to achieve your goals.

Brands: These are firms or individuals that own the product or service. The sectors are as diverse as you can imagine; retail, industry, financial services, travel, e-commerce, etc. Affiliate marketers that make the most money are affiliated with brands. They have been around for quite a while, and they understand the ins and outs of the market, and the brands can trust them for a great ROI. However, if you are starting out in affiliate marketing, best to stay away from brands, and work with affiliate networks.

Affiliates: The affiliate is the marketing partner of various brands. As an affiliate marketer, it is your job to win more customers for the product you are promoting and get compensated as per the agreement. The great thing about affiliate marketing is that you can still get started despite having little resources. For instance, if you have a blog, that's enough, and you can write reviews, post on social media, and direct your target audience to your affiliate links.

Affiliate marketing can also be an expensive job, as you may need a considerable budget in order to buy ad spaces and traffic. If you have the budget, and you are good at optimizing the campaigns, this combination would net you tremendous profits.

Affiliate Networks: An affiliate network pools together all brands that are looking to have their products and services promoted. And then affiliate marketers may sign up to these affiliate networks so they may promote the program that they feel they are sufficiently equipped to promote. Newbie affiliate marketers ought to sign up to affiliate networks so that they may have access to the numerous affiliate programs and thus get a chance to decide what they are best at promoting.

Affiliate networks also handle the tracking, reporting, and payments, meaning that the affiliate marketer won't have trouble claiming their earnings, as there is an established method of doing things. The affiliate marketer promotes the products or services of a brand with the primary aim of increasing business, and they get compensated as per their agreement with the affiliate network or brand.

Ways to Generate Traffic for your Affiliate Products

It is after the application process that the real work begins. Now that you have a product or service to promote, you can now start gathering traffic and funneling them towards your affiliate links. There are multiple methods on how you can do this.

The Paid Traffic Methods

First, you can use paid methods as a source of traffic. You can use advertising platforms that allow affiliate links and pay for the clicks or the views that you ad gets. With this method, you are spending money to make money. You will need a bankroll of hundreds, if not thousands of dollars to make this strategy work. You will also need to make sure that you follow the guidelines set by the affiliate advertisers.

Most of them will restrict you from using certain keywords in the advertising targeting. If you are selling Adidas wears for example, the affiliate program contract may restrict you from using the keywords like Adidas. They do this to prevent affiliate marketers from competing with the mother company in the advertising bidding.

Some other paid traffic methods include:

- Paid social media traffic from ads run social media like Facebook, Twitter, Instagram, Pinterest, LinkedIn, etc.
- Paid traffic from top search engines like Google and Bing.
- Paid traffic from native ad networks like Taboola, Outbrain, Rev content, Ad blade, etc.
- Traffic from solos ads (buying clicks from someone who has already-grown email list in your product niche).

Free Traffic Methods - Spreading the Affiliate Links around the Web

The second method of sending traffic is to spread the link around the web. Harness the power of social platforms like relevant Facebook groups, YouTube, Pinterest, LinkedIn, Quora, etc. to create large followings and get free traffic to your offers.

In the past, people used to do sleazy techniques to get clicks on their affiliate links. Some of them for instance, put their affiliate links in the signature part of their forum accounts. This way, when people see their forum comments, they also see the affiliate links. Many forums learned about this technique and now ban the use of links in the signature.

Some affiliate programs also allow the use of redirects and pop-ups to gather traffic. An affiliate marketer using redirect for example, may set up a page that will automatically redirect to the affiliate website. When the visitor visits that page, they are automatically transferred to the affiliate program's landing page. The problem with this strategy is that most people who go through the automatic redirect are sent to the affiliate program's website unwillingly. The majority of them will bounce. This excess traffic of non-buyers will eventually take its toll in the advertiser's website. This is the reason why many affiliate programs ban the use of redirects.

Some people also use link pop-ups to send people through the affiliate link. They may set the pop-up to appear after a certain link in the website is clicked. Upon clicking the said link, another window or tab will open. This works both for desktop and for mobile browsers. When the pop-up opens, the affiliate link is triggered and the affiliate landing page starts to load. This process of sending traffic to affiliate programs is also problematic. Aside from being prohibited by most affiliate programs, browsers also tend to have pop-up blocking technology. This prevents most of the pop-ups from opening even when the right link is clicked.

Content Marketing – The Best Method

The recommended way of gathering traffic for your affiliate programs is through the use of content marketing. Content marketing is simply the process of gathering internet user's attention by using different types of content media. One has the option of using text, audio, images, videos or a combination of all these to invite people to go to your website.

News websites are a classic example of websites that use content marketing. They create news articles and accompany them with videos and relevant images. After creating them, they post their content in their social media properties. They spread their news articles through Facebook, Twitter, and other social media marketing platforms. When a person interested in the news sees the article, the headline and the accompanying image should compel them to click on the link of the article. This will lead them to the news website.

After reading the article, they may press the up-vote button for the content. Some may even share a link of the content to their friends. By doing this, they are spreading the news and increasing the reach of the news article. Other people interested in the news may also click on the article. Afterwards they may also share the content with their own social media followers, continuing to spread the news. Some people who may be looking to read that specific news article may also go to Google and do a search. Because of proper search engine optimization practices, the article landed in the top spot of the search result page with its relevant keywords or key phrases. Because of this, more people from Google will read the content. Some of the readers who are interested in the content of the article may also choose to share it with their friends.

While this may seem like a simplistic illustration of how content marketing works, this is how it happens for most content on the web. Content creators simple make the content and share them in the relevant online hotspots. They develop their skill in getting people's attention over thousands of hours of practice.

You could also do the same with your affiliate marketing business. You could lure internet users to go to your website by creating and sharing content that are relevant to their interests and needs. In the process of viewing your content, they should also see the affiliate ads that you share in between your web pages. A percentage of them will click on these marketing materials and make a purchase. You will receive a percentage of the sale amount that your referred customers spend.

Email Marketing

This involves collecting interested users' active email with the main aim to notify them about new offers. The best way to capture interested users' email is through the use of landing pages.

A landing or squeeze page can be created as an informative article, or as a way to collect your site visitors' information, such as their active email address or phone number. You can create beautiful landing pages with software like clickfunnels, leadpages, instapages, etc. Landing pages will also enable you to install tracking pixels. These pixels can be very useful in order to retarget the visitors that did not purchase or opt in to your offer for a fraction of the price.

In my opinion, collecting emails should be a must for any affiliate marketer. What many marketers will tell you to do is to send traffic directly to the offer or to an advertorial, and although it is possible to make some money doing it that way, failing to create an email list could result in losing hundreds of thousands of dollars in the long run because you will not be creating a real business. I can't stress enough about the importance of growing an email list. Many people don't do this because growing an email list can take more time, but trust me, you will be glad that you did it.

A customer's email list, when used correctly, is used to interact, help, and generate trust with people. It is not another way to spam them with unrelated offers every day or sell them on crappy products. Once you grow your list to a few thousand members, it will become a great asset to your business because you will no longer have to rely on paid traffic to reach potential customers.

How Does an Email List Work?

Let's say that you promote a product on the weight loss niche. In order to get people into your list, you must first target them with a free offer (also known as "lead magnet"). This could be a free report on anything that people will be interested in. Your free offer should provide good information and add value to their lives. Also, the image used should portray something worth giving away an email address for.

Once you have your free offer ready, you will then send traffic to a landing page created with the sole purpose to encourage visitors to exchange their active email addresses for the free report. Your goal is to get as many people to subscribe to your list as possible, because once they do, you can continue to reach out to them without having to purchase traffic from expensive traffic sources.

Note that creating an email list should not be solely to make money without adding value to your subscribers' lives. You should be dedicated to truly help these people with their problems. If you do this right, your subscribers will always patronize the products and services you recommend. In return, you will make not only really good commission, but some of your subscribers will also invite their friends to join your email list, thereby helping to grow your list for free.

Check: 12 Tips to Help You Build an Efficient Email Marketing Contact List at
https://www.buzzingpoint.com/2020/04/build-email-marketing-contact-list.html

Other Important Affiliate Marketing Tools

Click Trackers

You can track your ad clicks with a click tracker. A good click tracker helps you to collect data in order to scale your campaigns quicker. It enables you to keep count of the percentage of people that saw your ads and clicked on it and probably the percentage that actually purchased the product you are promoting. If you are running multiple ads on the same or different ad platforms, click trackers provide a great way to find out which ad or landing page performs the best, so as to know which ad to concentrate on.

Some of the recommended click trackers include:

- Clickmagick
- Voluum
- Clickmeter
- Cpvlab

If you are serious about getting started with affiliate marketing, a link tracker is a great tool. It can help you make the best financial decision faster.

An autoresponder is a program that allows you to setup messages that go out automatically to people who have subscribed to your email list. These messages are sent depending on the order that the subscribers signed up, but you are can control how frequent these messages go out to your list. I usually set my autoresponders to send one email a day from Sunday through Thursday. For an autoresponder to work, you must provide an email list beforehand. Autoresponders are very necessary if you wish to automate your communication with your subscribers and probably make money while you sleep.

There are thousands of autoresponder programs available for business marketing, but unfortunately, most of them are not very reliable. You need to choose an efficient one. The first autoresponder I personally recommend is **Getrespons**e - very beginner friendly and has active and reliable support team. Other good autoresponders are **Aweber** and **MailChimp**.

MailChimp

Email marketing is one of the best marketing channels. Marketing through an email list is up to four times more profitable than display ads. But then email marketing software doesn't come cheap, especially if you are a newbie. But thank goodness, you can sign up to MailChimp and build your email list for free up to 2000 subscribers. Beyond that mark, you will start paying, but more often than not, you will be making some decent money.

Google Ads Display Network

If you are into buying ads, you want to be aware of your ads' performance. Failure to study the performance of your ads can very well lead to tremendous losses. But when you are aware of what is taking place, you are in a position to keep changing your ads and ensuring that your campaign is profitable. Engaging in media buying is one of the best ways to scale your campaign profitability. However, if you do it poorly, you are bound to suffer major losses.

Bing Ad Center

For some reason, when people talk about media buying, the only platform that seems to hit them is Google. Most people forget that even Bing is a powerful tool that could help you run profitable campaigns. Using the Bing ad center, you are in a position to determine the performance of your ads, and this allows you to run profitable campaigns.

PPC Web Spy

As an affiliate marketer, you have to keep your opponents close. You have to find out what they are up to. When you are aware of the keywords that your competitors are bidding for, it gives you the inspiration to benefit from competition. The PPC web spy allows you to track the keywords your competitors are using.

Google Alerts

In order to optimize your campaigns, you need to know what your target audience is up to. One of the ways to understand what your audience is up to is through setting up Google alerts. First, come up with phrases that you are targeting and set up the alerts. For instance, you might target blogs and forums, and once your target audience uses those phrases, you get notified and engage them.

Backtweets

As an affiliate marketer, you want to keep tabs on everyone who is talking about you. You cannot afford to ignore it. If they are saying nice things, appreciate them, but if they are tarnishing your name, you might want to seek clarification and correct their misjudgment. One of the best platforms that allow people to manage their reputation is Twitter. But then you cannot view all the tweets about you at random. With the help of a back tweet, you are in a position to view every last tweet about you and get to make quick decisions.

Brandwatch

As an affiliate marketer, your key interest is working with the best brands. But then you cannot understand what brand is the best without the proper understanding of what they are like. Thus, you need to be in a position to understand what is being said about all these brands. Brandwatch will help you to keep track of what people are saying about various brands. Through brand watch, you are in a position to decide the best brands to partner with.

Pinterest Business Analytics

Pinterest is one of the most used marketing tools. Customers have been found to be responsive to high-quality images. Thus, ensure you are using a Pinterest account to push your marketing message. The Pinterest business analytics should help you keep track of the traffic you are receiving and how your customers interact with your products.

SocialMention

You also want to be aware of the trends. When you are aware of the trends, you are in a position to take advantage of these trends and develop a campaign to your advantage. SocialMention will help you keep tabs of the various trends that have emerged, and you will be in a position to maximize your earning capacity.

On-page Optimization Tool

In order to attract the largest crowd of targeted customers, you need to have a strong on-page optimization game. When your website is very well optimized, it means that the search engines will give it top rank, and as a result, people will easily discover the website, and with more visibility, the sales conversions shoot through the roof.

YouTube Keyword Tool

Video marketing is the in-thing nowadays. In actual fact, it is projected to take center stage in the coming years. Thus, it is incredibly important that you create awesome videos and seed them with relevant keywords so that you may maximize your earning potential. Using the YouTube keyword tool, you are in a position to determine the best keywords for your videos.

Image SEO Tool

You also need to understand that images play a key role in boosting the performance of your marketing. Customers seem to respond greatly to marketing messages that feature high-quality images. The Image SEO tool helps with improving image quality and thus promoting the profitability of your marketing campaign.

Alexa

This tool by Amazon is awesome for analyzing how you are faring against your competition. It allows you to gauge your traffic and also the tendencies of your visitors. The free version is limited, but once you become a paying customer, you have the opportunity to see powerful metrics.

Canva

This tool helps marketers create awesome images and design powerful templates. With Canva, there's no limit to your creativity; you have semi-finished templates to work with, and the outcome is nothing short of spectacular.

The Best Recommended Affiliate Programs

As an affiliate marketer, your success is, to a large extent, dependent upon the affiliate program you choose. Although there is no standard way to find out the best programs, but the main thing is to check the commission rate and the program's policies. With all these factors considered, here are some affiliate programs I recommend:

eCommerce Affiliate Programs:

- BigCommerce
- Weebly
- 3DCART
- Shopify
- Wix
- CJ Affiliate
- ShareSale
- Amazon Associates
- eBay Partner Network
- ClickBank

Travel Affiliate Programs:

- TripAdvisor
- TravelPayouts

- Expedia
- SkyScanner
- Agoda
- Booking.com
- Airbnb

Dating Affiliate Programs:

- Cupid Media
- People Media
- Match.com
- EHarmony
- Elite Singles

Web Hosting Affiliate Programs:

- WP Engine
- Liquid Web
- Cloudways
- SiteGround
- Kinsta

Educational Affiliate Programs:

- Coursera
- Udemy
- Skillshare
- DIY.org
- Teachable

Gaming Affiliate Programs:

- Razer
- LogiTech
- Alienware
- Nvidia
- Microsoft

Things to Consider when Choosing an Affiliate Program

As an affiliate marketer, you must realize that you are filling in an important gap. You are playing a key role in growing a business and improving the economy at large. But then you need to be mindful of yourself. You need to be careful about the programs that you sign up for. The following are some of the things you should consider when selecting an affiliate program.

Commissions

Depending on the product, and the effort you are expected to make, always ensure that the program is offering decent commissions. There are very many programs out there out to oppress the affiliate marketer, and unless you are alert, you wouldn't even know. Always look at the commissions and, if possible, try to find evidence that they actually pay out these earnings. But then you shouldn't be only money-minded. You have to perform the risk-benefit analysis. If an affiliate program pays little commissions, justified by the fact that it's far easier to get leads and sales in that niche, it makes more sense to take it up as opposed to a program that pays out hefty commissions while it's nearly impossible to get any conversion.

Affiliate Cookie Lifespan

When you become an affiliate marketer, you are given a trackable link that makes it possible to rightly credit your conversions. The technology that makes this possible is known as a cookie. The longer your affiliate cookie, the better for you, meaning that you increase your chances of getting more conversions credited to you. Assuming that an affiliate cookie had a 24-hour lifespan, it means that your target clients who interacted with your affiliate link have up to 24-hours to convert else you lose out. Ensure that you work with programs that have a considerable affiliate cookie lifespan.

Brand Recognition

Generally, it is much easier to sell products that are fairly recognized as opposed to products that are totally new. Ensure that you are marketing a product that is fairly popular, for it has garnered a bit of traction, making your work easier. But this is not to mean you must shun every product that people aren't particularly familiar with. Sometimes you may come upon a product that you will instinctually feel has a lot of potential as a newcomer, and it would be just as great to put your efforts into marketing this product. But in general, terms, ensure you are marketing fairly popular brands.

Merchant/Network Transparency

The first sign of a suspicious merchant or network is ambiguity. They hide important information instead of highlighting it. This is deliberate because they are expecting to confound you when their unfair practices come to light. Ensure that you are familiar with their terms and conditions. Failure to assess a merchant or affiliate network amounts to negligence on your part, and it could turn out to be an expensive mistake.

Consider Niche Alignment

There might be a low barrier to entry into any affiliate program, but it doesn't change the fact that you are more likely to perform whilst promoting a product/service in your circle of competence. And people can always tell if you know what you are talking about or if you are a poser. For that reason, it is important to ensure that the affiliate program you select aligns with your niche.

How to Find a Profitable Affiliate Marketing Niche

One of the factors that allow you to earn huge commissions is through selecting the right niches. The following are some important steps for selecting the best niche.

Brainstorm

You'd be surprised how the people around you could assist you in choosing the best niche. Ensure that you have something in common. This allows you to have an easy time deciding on the perfect niche.

Identify your Challenges

Start looking at all the things troubling you all. Where there's a challenge, there's a money-making opportunity. You have to be honest with yourself in order to ensure you may come up with the best niche.

Select the most Profitable Problem

For instance, if you are a young adult, one of the problems you might be having is money, or more specifically, how to make money online. Now, you could decide to promote a platform that allows young people to make money online. This becomes so much easier to promote because you have a wealth of information that will help you promote the product.

Understand the Problem

Just because you are aware of the problem doesn't mean it's enough. Commit to understanding the problem in a much deeper way so that you can know how to make the most of the situation.

Things to Consider When Choosing a Profitable Niche

The following are some of the vital things to consider when selecting a profitable niche.

Market Value

It is important to enter a niche with substantial market data. This allows you to be able to estimate your earning potential. Generally, you want to stick with niches with a high market value. When the market value is high, it shows that the customers are responsive to the products, and this allows you to make more money.

Past and Current Trends

By studying past and current trends, you are giving yourself the chance to predict what could happen in the future. Studying past and current niche trends allow you to be comfortable in your decisions and to forecast what may happen. Analyzing the past and current trends promote your creativity and empower you to make the most of the situation.

Understand the Problems of your Niche

It is important to accurately understand the problem that is going on in your niche. When you have a clear understanding of the problem, you have a decent chance of turning things to your favor. But when you don't understand the problem thoroughly, you are more likely to lose out.

Audience Passion

Passion is one factor that pushes us into taking certain actions. You want to ask yourself whether your audience is passionate enough to convert into customers. You have to pick an affiliate program that will be received well. This allows you to make money. However, if your target audience has little to zero passion for your product, obviously, your earning potential will be greatly compromised.

Target Audience Spending Power

You also need to understand that promoting a niche isn't enough, but your target audience should have the means to buy whatever you are promoting. Passion alone is not enough. Thus, if you are promoting a product which price tag is beyond the ability of the target audience, it doesn't matter that they need the product, but still, they won't have the capacity to buy.

Nature of the Products

As an affiliate marketer, you will be promoting products of a different nature. You want to select a niche whose products can be handled well by your audience. For instance, if you are promoting products to an audience in a third world country, it is far more profitable to sell informational products, as opposed to tangible products because the infrastructure to receive these goods might be lacking.

Competition

Some niches tend to be particularly competitive. Do you have the potential to withstand this competition? Ensure that you are adequately prepared; otherwise, look for a niche where there's less competition. This is especially so if you don't have the budget to sustain a powerful campaign. But also ensure that you develop your strength so that you won't always have to shun competition. It is important that you develop your content and strengthen your marketing game so that you may increase your profits and establish your presence as a thought leader.

How to Define your Niche Market

The affiliate marketer needs to narrow down their target audience. You don't possibly have the resources and capital to market and sell a wide range of products. Thus, it is important that you stick to a sizable target audience so that you may be able to maximize your earnings. The following is a step-by-step process of defining your niche market.

Create a Wish List

The first step is to find out precisely the entities that you want to do business with. This means you have to be as specific as possible. For instance, if you are marketing software, don't lunge at every software company that you come across on the internet. Instead, concentrate on software companies within a certain locale, and that generate a certain amount of income. This ensures that you stay focused and deliver quality products. The market is always too big, and an affiliate marketer is never enough to satisfy the needs of that market.

Acknowledge your Resources

In order to be a successful marketer, you have to make the best use of your resources. You have to be honest with yourself about your capabilities and the distance you are willing to go in order to turn up a profit. If you are not honest with yourself, you will end up hijacking your potential and affect the success of your marketing campaigns. But when you are honest with yourself about the resources you have, it increases your capacity to grow your business.

Bring Out the X Factor

Almost any niche you can think of, you are going to face competition. But if you have the X factor, you are always going to stand out. Ensure that you always have the X factor. This means that you should have great appeal and show your target audience that you are offering something they cannot live without. The X factor makes you stand out and look like someone who's well aware of what they are doing. In order to stand out, ensure that you think through your business model, and find out the needs you are going to be fulfilling with the product or service that you are promoting. Failure to think through your business model might deny you success.

Test your Marketing Campaigns

In as much as you believe in your capacity to succeed while promoting certain goods and services to a certain target audience, don't be overconfident. Overconfidence can lead you to incur tremendous losses. Ensure that you always test your campaigns in order to ensure that you are running a profitable campaign.

Affiliate Marketing Keyword Research Tips

Keyword research is an important thing. You need to be thorough about it so that you might scale the profitability of your campaign. The following are some incredible tips on how to perform keyword research.

Know your Customers

You want to be the type of person who understands precisely who you are looking to attract. For that reason, you must put extra effort into identifying your target audience. Ensure that you are aware of your target audience at all times. Knowing your customers means that you must be willing to put the extra effort into identifying the sort of people that surround you and understand what they are hoping to get from you. There are various tools to help you target your customers well and make the best use of that opportunity. Always ensure that you are well-versed with the kind of people you are dealing with, and this should help you come up with the right keywords.

Analyze the Keywords you are Targeting

Don't be too hasty in choosing a keyword. Always take your time to understand the best keyword for you so that you might be able to optimize your campaigns. There are many tools that make it possible to analyze keywords and ensure that things are in order. Take advantage of these keywords and ensure that everything is in order. Through proper analysis of keywords, you are in a position to understand the ones that suit your business and business model most. However, when you don't engage in keyword analysis, you deny yourself the chance to witness the best possible results, and this could greatly hinder you from running a successful marketing campaign.

Analyze your Competitor

In the early days of the internet, the competition was pretty low, considering people were busy being creative and diversifying the markets, and that not too many people had ventured into making the internet dollar. However, at the present moment, as an affiliate marketer, you have got to be pretty aggressive. This means you have to keep looking at what your competitors are doing. Be that person who's aware of the things that your competitors are up to. In that sense, you will have the capacity to position yourself so as to win against the competition. If you fail to watch your competitors, you are going to greatly water down the effectiveness of your marketing, and in worse cases, fail to make a profit.

Rank for Special Features

Understand all the special features at your disposal and try to rank for them. In this way, you have to be willing to look at the best feature of your marketing campaigns and use all the tools at your disposal to highlight these features. By so doing, you increase your capacity to attract more targeted customers to your affiliate links.

Position Keywords Appropriately

Ensure that you put the keywords in the right places. This will ensure that your marketing message is very well propagated and that the search engines will rank your content very highly, and as a result, there'll be valuable customers landing on your page. Some marketers get the keyword-positioning off, and this contributes to the failure of their marketing campaigns.

However, if you manage to get it right, which means if you manage to seed the keywords naturally within your marketing content, you are in a position to boost your profits and run successful campaigns. On the other hand, if you don't understand how to place keywords, you are at risk of sabotaging the profitability of your marketing campaigns.

How to Study your Competitors

You certainly don't want to be the sort of person who says they are doing their own thing and fail to watch what their competitors are up to. You want to be the person who keeps an eye on what your competitors are doing. When it comes to studying your competitors, the following are some of the things you should keep in mind.

Go beyond Google Search

For most people, Google is the first thing they turn to when they want to find out about their competitors. But then Google is not enough. In as much as you can learn a lot from the information seeded in Google, there's still a lot more to learn by using targeted tools. Ensure that you use tools that help you take a closer analysis of Google's results. There are various tools in the market to help you develop a keen understanding of your competitors. Once you have more understanding of what your competitors are up to, you develop the inspiration to improve your marketing campaigns.

Look at their Social Media Handles

Your competitors aren't only seeding content in search engines like Google. There's a lot more they are saying on their fan pages on social media. You want to follow and like them so that you may understand what is going on in their lives. Social media will allow you to see the various vulnerabilities of your competitors, considering the fact that it promotes a "loose" environment. By keeping track of what your competitors are saying on Social Media, you are in a position to guess their train of thoughts, and thus it gives you the inspiration to improve the success of your marketing campaign.

Ask your Customers

Your new customers might very well be wonderful sources of information about your competitors. When you bag a new customer, just reach out to them and find out whom they had been transacting with before, and why they decided to cross over. Ensure that your questions are well formatted so that it might seem natural, or else you will cause the customers to get on guard. Never fail to engage your customers. Always ensure that you provide quality services and products to your customers so that you may have an enabling environment for feedback.

Work with People who know about your Competitors

Another way to acquire valuable information about your competitors is by working with people who have insider knowledge, particularly former employees of your competitors. They might have left their former employers in good or bad terms, but that is irrelevant; once they come on board they are supposed to help you get to the very top, and revealing critical information about their former employers is part of the deal, but then you don't want to act pushy about it. You certainly must ensure that you are respectful.

How to Discover Good Products to Promote

As an affiliate marketer, you want to promote the best products so that you might maximize your profits. In the world of affiliate marketing, identifying great products is not as easy as one might think, because they are subjective. In other words, what might strike you as difficult to promote could very well be easy to promote for another person. But with that stated, here are some of the factors you must consider when selecting the best product to promote.

Utility

At the end of the day, people won't be merely spending money for the heck of it. They are spending money on products and services to serve a certain function. Thus, ensure you well understand the functionality of the product or service you are promoting. The more usable a product or service, the more receptive the market is going to be. You don't want to promote products and services that no one has used for. To determine the utility of a product, ensure that you look at your target audience, and gauge how your product and service could help solve their problems.

Maintainability

Everything fashioned by the human mind is subject to flaws. Nothing created by a human being is ever immortal. But in the same breath, there is a need for creating something with a considerable shelf-life, and that is easy to maintain. Products that require easy maintenance are more resourceful than products that require high maintenance.

Price

At the end of the day, people must part with their money in order to grant them the service or product. This means, if you are poor at matching up your target audience with the appropriate offer, you could very well incur untold losses. Always go for the products and services that are appropriately priced. This should boost your marketing and help you enjoy more sales.

Ease of use

Also, ensure that you are working with products that are easy to use. People are looking for simplicity. Their day to day lives are already complex. Thus, the simpler you make your products and services, the easier it becomes to attract customers and increase your profits. But if something is difficult to use, then more people are repelled.

Mass Appeal

Some brands have mass appeal as opposed to other brands even though they handle products and services in a similar niche. Thus, you have got to use this to your advantage. Ensure that you are promoting products and services that most people are happy to associate with. This makes easy work on the promotion part. However, if you start marketing products and services that most people don't like, then you are obviously going to have a hard time making a profit.

Different Ways to Make Money from Affiliate Marketing

There are many strategies you can use to start making money in affiliate marketing. I have tried many affiliate marketing strategies. The 2 strategies I will reveal below gave me the best result. For the first strategy, you will need an active blog or website.

First Strategy

Here you will need to have a popular or active blog or website that gets its traffic mainly from social media and search engines. Now research and discover products with very high demand. Write a detailed review about the product. Optimize the review article so that it ranks high on search engines. Add your affiliate link within the article content and set it to open in a new tab.

See: Blog SEO - How to Optimize your Posts to Rank #1 on Search Engines at
https://www.buzzingpoint.com/2020/05/blog-seo-how-to-optimize-blog.html

Now share the review across various social media platforms, especially, Facebook, Pinterest, Twitter, Instagram, and Quora.

You can even run paid traffic ad campaigns for the article. But make sure the campaign setup is in line with the policies of the affiliate network. Most of them require that you don't use the brand name as ad keywords.

Use ad trackers to check the performance of the paid ads, so as to make sure your ROI is high. You might need to create multiple ad campaigns and then compare their performance.

If you have push notification setup for your blog or email subscribers, you can notify them about the new product review articles. When these blog audience read the article, they will discover the product. Now because the product has high demand, many of them will be interested to buy it.

Make sure you choose the product with a comparatively low price so as to entice them the more. Once they click on the link, it will direct them to the product page. Once they buy the product, you earn your commission.

Second Strategy

It all starts with traffic. You need to first channel traffic to a landing page containing your free offer in order to collect email addresses from your site visitors. This traffic should come from your favourite traffic source. Once visitors arrive at your landing page and enter their email address in exchange for the free offer, their email address will immediately enter your autoresponders database, where you have a pre-written sequence of emails that will be sent to these subscribers.

Once the subscribers submit the email, they will be redirected to your "thank you" or pre-sell page, where they will be pre-framed so that they can purchase your product at a low cost or be given more information about your business.

Using the weight loss niche as example, you can give away a free report on the top 10 foods to avoid in order to lose weight quickly. Once the subscribers submit their information, they will be redirected to a "Thank you" page where you will recommend a $5 natural detox guide or provide further information that will contribute to the value of your product.

The sales copy on the "Thank you" page can be something like:

"*Thank you, I have sent the free email provided. You will receive it in a few minutes. While you wait, here are some benefits of a natural detox...*"

Proceed to explain the benefits. After the explanation, you can now recommend a $5 step by step detox guide (this is the affiliate product you are promoting) written by an experience nutritionist.

Additionally, you can provide your subscribers with another free offer that complements the original offer. For example, after the subscribers have claimed the free report, you can offer them free access to your Facebook group, ask them to subscribe to your YouTube channel. This is a strategy to further utilize the leads. It also helps you to recoup some of the money invested on paid traffic and even earn more income.

Affiliate Marketing Tips and Tricks

To an extent, the difference between successful and unsuccessful affiliate marketers might be down to knowledge. The more an affiliate knows about their trade, the easier it becomes for them to run successful marketing campaigns. There are many affiliate marketing tips and tricks to help marketers become successful. Thus, a marketer must never tire of digging up new trends and acquiring new ideas on how they may maximize their earnings. The following are some important affiliate marketing tips and tricks.

Know Your Audience

Ensure that you have complete understanding of the people that you are targeting. When you have complete understanding of your target audience, it allows you to utilize the right marketing channels, and run winning campaigns. When you have complete understanding of your audience, you have tremendous power and it helps you scale the profitability of your marketing campaign. Knowing your audience comes down to having great understanding of your product and understanding what need it fulfills or what problem it solves. It is also critical to use great tools to help you capture important information about your target audience. In this way, you have the capacity to understand what your target audience is truly about.

Be Trustworthy

Nothing would get your customers to run away from you as fast as cheating them. And make no mistake about it. There's no little trick you can pull to make your customers blind to the fact that you have scammed them. Some affiliate marketers are not necessarily scammers in the sense of cheating their customer out of their money, but rather, they simply fail to meet expectations. The affiliate marketer might send out an inflated advertising message, and once the customer is hooked, they later find out that the product or service is far different than what was advertised, thus they have a bad impression of that business. Always ensure that you are sending out accurate information.

Be Kind

Being kind means that you have to treat your customers with patience. You must not act entitled. When you approach your target customers with a stinking attitude it will only serve to send them the opposite direction. But when you are kind it shows in how you talk to and interact with your customers. People will be genuinely happy around you. When you are a kind business person, it builds your reputation, and your customers take it upon themselves to promote your business. On the other hand, when you are hostile and inconsiderate, people will keep a wide berth from you.

Be Transparent About Affiliate Relationships

Don't try to position yourself as the creator of a product or service when you are clearly not. Some affiliate marketers think too highly of themselves and they can't help but deceive their audiences. Well, this is what you have to understand. You cannot deceive people for long. Eventually, they catch up with you, and the consequences are quite bitter. Thus, ensure you are disclosing your affiliate relationships so that your target audience might know you are just a marketer and not the creator of the product or service.

Select Affiliate Products Carefully

One of the most important factors for success in affiliate marketing is selecting the best product. Ensure that you consider your abilities before you decide to promote a product or service. For instance, if you have a background in finance, you are in a position to make great headway by promoting finance-related products. But if you have a background in real estate, you would do great promoting real estate products. But then affiliate marketing allows people to promote the products they have always wanted. So, it is not a must you have a related background, you only need passion, but then you need to be aware of how your product selection sits with your resources. For instance, if you run a blog that educates pregnant women on how to lose weight, it makes sense to promote health-related products as opposed to financial products.

Try Different Programs

You don't want to work with the same program or merchant all the time. Most successful affiliate marketers have worked with different merchants and affiliate networks. This helps them weed out the low-quality merchants and affiliate networks and stick with those that bring in the best results. At present, you can gauge the effectiveness of an affiliate network by checking out their reviews on internet forums. If the networks are scamming affiliate marketers, you will surely know about it, and if the networks are incredibly great for marketers, you will still know. Thus, ensure you are trying out many different networks.

Write Ever-green Content

One of the best channels for marketing products and services is the use of website content. If you want to attract customers through search engines for the long haul, you need to create quality ever-green content. Thus, ensure you write timeless content. When you have quality content, it ranks top on search engines, and that way people will always be clicking on your affiliate links. Also, ensure that you have a simple writing style. This means you must refrain from big words and stick to the language that even a kid would understand.

Be Patient

For some crazy reason, newbie affiliate marketers imagine they can receive their first paycheck within one week of trying out affiliate marketing. It doesn't work that way. In order to become successful in affiliate marketing, you need to put in the work, and this means you might go for a while without seeing positive results, depending on the niche that you select. Affiliate marketers who are not patient are likely to act out randomly and water down the effectiveness of their marketing campaigns. But when one is patient they have the capacity to put in the work and wait until the fruit is ripe.

Increase the Visibility of your Website

Having a website is not enough. It should also rank well. After all, what's the use in having a website that is ranked page three or worse? It takes tremendous hard work to get your website to rank on top search results. Apart from creating amazing content, ensure that you also engage in content promotion, so that there might be links pointing back to your website and increase its ranking. Also, ensure that you have mastered keyword research so that you might be able to attract super-targeted customers to your website.

Gain a Great Understanding of your Competitors

Don't turn away from them. By watching what they are up to, you gain inspiration on how to tackle them. However, if you don't watch your competition, they might get the better of you and kill your business. Another way to increase your website visibility is through SEO. Ensure that your website has great SEO – both on-page and off-page. Increasing your website's visibility, or in other words outranking your competition, comes down to being a hard worker, and staying consistent with your marketing efforts.

Optimize Your Website for Mobile Users

If your website is not mobile-friendly, you are leaving a lot of money on the table. You are literally throwing money away. Ensure that at all times your website is optimized for mobile. And this is simply because more people the world over are accessing the internet via mobile devices as opposed to PCs. Thus, when you make your website mobile friendly, people will easily engage with your content and convert into paying customers. On the other hand, if your website is not optimized for mobile traffic, then mobile users will abandon your website and walk right into the arms of your competitors.

Create an Engaging Discussion

If you want to be truly successful for the long-term, your aim shouldn't be only turning a visitor into a customer and then tossing them away. You need to create a family so that every last of your customers may feel as though they belong. This ensures that you have a tight family of customers who are ever ready to contribute positively. With the existence of social media, you can create fan pages, and ask your customers to subscribe, and then come up with interesting threads so that your customers may contribute. The more you do this, the easier it becomes to promote awareness, and such an activity improves your reputation.

However, if you have a tendency of discarding your customers, they will have no incentive of turning back to you when they need a similar product or service. Thus, ensure that you are always engaging your customers so that you may be able to improve customer loyalty.

Don't Rely on a Single Traffic Source

One of the major mistakes that affiliate marketers do is always relying on one traffic source. This is incredibly risky. Normally, when an affiliate marketer is starting out, they have a tendency of trying out many things, and sometimes they have the bad luck of setting up campaigns that are not profitable, but once they hack a combination that works, they stay faithful to that traffic source even when the offers change. The fact is that different traffic sources are excellent for different affiliate offers. And for that reason, you cannot afford to tie yourself down to a single traffic source.

You need to keep testing various traffic sources and eventually you will gain deep insight as to what traffic sources work best for various affiliate offers.

Always Research

You don't have to be the victim of poor decisions anymore. We have the internet now. If you are not sure about something, you only have to log on to the internet and eliminate your doubts. By always conducting research you are in a position to improve the efficiency of your marketing. Apart from running researching via Google, you also have social media groups comprised of people that share similar philosophies, and such people would be tremendous help in the research process. Do I mean to say that you can go to a Facebook group and pose a question and expect great answers? Yes! But then observe the rules of decency and respect. Also, there are many question and answer websites that should help you gather the knowledge you are looking for.

As a Beginner, Start with Affordable Tools

When one is a newbie, it's not like they have a bottomless well of resources from which they can fund their marketing campaigns. Newbies need to use their resources wisely in order to run successful marketing campaigns. One of the ways to run successful campaigns is through ensuring they use free or freemium tools. This allows them to save resources. If you have a small budget you want to use Freemium tools in your marketing so that you may be able to extend your run. However, once a newbie starts to pull in the dough, it is necessary that they invest in great marketing tools, for this will greatly scale the profitability of their marketing campaigns.

Stay in Touch with Peers

If you can work the courage to drop your ego and work together, your peers can be a great source of knowledge on what works in your industry. But then you want to be careful that you don't drop all your secrets for that would be akin to selling yourself out. But then it is beneficial that both parties help one another out. At the end of the day, when you exchange information, that's a mutually beneficial arrangement. You cannot possibly know everything. Thus, it is important that peers exchange relevant information.

Have Self-Belief

It might seem cliché, but it is incredibly important. You should always think highly of yourself. You should consider yourself to possess the power to achieve your marketing goals. If you are not psychologically prepared for success, it can become very difficult to achieve your goals. Self-belief stems from having self-awareness and feeding your mind with positivity. Of course, you will meet disappointments, but you must condition yourself to overcome these disappointments and attain success.

Believe in the Product

Apart from having self-belief, it is also important to believe in the product. This means that you should take the extra step of using the product so that you already what it feels like to use these product or service. Of course you cannot possibly use every product or service you will promote. But generally, once you have understood what a product is like, you are likely to be more passionate, and this should drive more sales.

If you use a product and realize that it's a flop, remember you are responsible of your customers, so it is wise to drop the product and look for an alternative. For instance, if you run a health fitness blog, and you are marketing a supplement, and upon trying this supplement you find out that it is low-quality, you need to do away with it.

Organize your Products

You don't want to be the person that runs a disorganized affiliate marketing business. You need to be aware of all your products and have them in an orderly fashion. For one, you need to have your products in a product table, and this will help you know the exact products you are promoting, and also it will help you perform an analysis on the products that are performing well as opposed to those that are performing poorly. When you organize your products you are in a position to optimize your campaigns and achieve great profits.

Create Engaging Content

One major characteristic of great content is that it has been broken down into easy-to follow steps. Thus, when you are creating content, ensure that it is well broken down, so that people may engage with the content pretty easily. Highly engaging content is an important factor in boosting sales conversions.

Encourage Referrals

It might immediately seem to be the case, but word of mouth is a tremendous form of marketing. If you have a website, never tire of reminding your audience to always refer your website to your friends. People are wont to take seriously what they have been told by their friends. Thus, encourage your customers to spread positive vibes about your business and in no time you will achieve tremendous sales.

Comply with the Laws

Don't be one of those people that like bending the law. There's no need to. Ensure that you are always operating within the laws without having to take advantage of your customers. For one, you have to disclose the fact that you have an affiliate relationship with a network or merchant and that you are gaining monetary benefits. You also have to be frank in your reviews and avoid exaggerating in an attempt to pull the customer in and get them to convert. Failure to comply with affiliate marketing laws could not only send your customers the opposite way but it could very well land you in trouble with the authorities. So, always ensure that you have that in mind.

Have a Learning Mindset

Never go into affiliate marketing thinking that you have all the answers, because you don't. Just ensure that you are always aware of what is taking place and have the sense to take advantage of trends that are advantageous to you. When you see trends that are really paying off, ensure that you take advantage of them, and as time goes, you will start reaping huge benefits.

Another aspect of having a learner's mindset is ensuring that you keep in touch with your peers. Never mislead yourself into thinking that you can do it alone. Trust me, you can't. You have to have the mindset of someone who's looking for new ways to improve their economic situation and you must never tire of improving your status.

Also, there is an ocean of classified affiliate marketing information on various membership sites and you might want to join those sites and see what they can do for you. This will go a long way in ensuring that you have the best tips on increasing your earnings.

Use Affiliate Tools

Don't be the type of person who's so economical that they don't value any affiliate marketing tool. Generally, when you deploy tools as part of your marketing arsenal, you are in a position to increase sales conversions, and run profitable marketing campaigns. Always ensure that you are using powerful tools to improve your marketing game. There are both free and paid affiliate marketing tools. Ensure that you work within your budget. You certainly don't want to constrain yourself too hard that you cannot perform anything else.

Track your Results

Ensure that you are always tracking your results. You don't want to have the wrong approach in business and end up ruining everything else. Ensure that you are always following to see how your marketing campaigns are faring. In this way, you will be in a position to determine the profitability of your marketing campaigns.

When you track your results, you are in a position to determine what is not working well for you, and this gives you the power to make necessary changes so that you might be able to run profitable campaigns. You will find that most successful affiliate marketers are heavily invested in tracking their results. And this tendency not only saves them thousands of dollars but it helps them optimize their campaigns so that they may maximize their earnings.

Check your Website for Errors

There are many things that could affect the proper functioning of your website, key among virus attacks. Thus, it is important to perform regular checks on the state of your website. This will help you repair your website and ensure everything runs smoothly. When you check your website for errors on a regular basis, you boost the efficient running of your business, and this boosts your conversion rates. On the other hand, when you desert your website, there's a chance it might get bugged, and then lead into performance problems, and this could affect the profitability of your marketing campaigns.

Don't Be Blinded By Payouts

Some affiliate marketers are so blinded by the commissions that they won't stop to look at other equally important factors and then they end up making poor choices. It is always important to select the best affiliate program overall. Thus, ensure that you take your time to select an affiliate program.

Invest in a Great Website

You don't want to be one of those people who create cheap websites and then wonder why they cannot pull in search engine traffic. In as much as quality is the number one determinant of high search engine ranking, we cannot wish away the technical aspect of things. The fact is marketers who invest in powerful and expensive webhosts and generally arm their websites with great tools are in a much better position to rank higher as opposed to marketers who slap together a $5 website and upload substandard content. When you have a professionally done website, sales conversions are definitely going up, because customers consider websites to be a key indicator of what type of person they are transacting with.

Learn from Successful Marketers

Successful affiliate marketers can help you climb your way to success too. But you have to be careful about how you approach it. You certainly don't want to come out of nowhere and claim to want the successful affiliate marketer to coach you into becoming a successful affiliate marketer; that reeks of entitlement. You need to first offer value to the top affiliate marketer and then once you have a relationship you should position yourself as a learner and get the successful affiliate marketer to show you the ropes. By learning from the best you are equipped with all the tricks on how to beat the odds and achieve the success you have always desired.

One of the easiest ways to get the attention of these top affiliate marketers in your niche is by visiting their websites and dropping helpful and meaningful tips in the comment section. Once you have dropped enough useful comments, contact the top marketer via email. Get in touch with him from time to time. With time, he will freely reveal some marketing tips that has helped him attain that great height in affiliate marketing.

Focus on Being Helpful

One of the reasons why most affiliate marketers fail to run a successful business is simply because they are obsessed about converting sales. Well, that's the wrong approach. An affiliate marketer should just obsess about being helpful to people. You should be looking to help people make the right choices and alleviate their problems. This mindset causes people to become sold on your products and they come away thinking highly of you.

When you are helpful, you are in a position to attract more people to your business, and build your reputation. Here's the thing. Everyone is looking to fulfill their important needs. No one really cares about the next person.

Thus, when you are helpful you are indirectly stroking their ego, and they will return the favor by becoming loyal customers.

Keep an Eye on Frauds

If you are not careful, you could very easily fall victim to an affiliate scam. You could run into an outfit that portrays itself as an affiliate network when it's really a solo scammer in a third world country looking to make some little money off of you.

One of the common characteristics across all affiliate network scams is that they rarely communicate. They will take forever to reply to your emails. And once you learn about their dirty little scheme they swiftly block you. Affiliate scammers have got to be some of the most cold-hearted humans out there.

Costly Mistakes that New Affiliate Marketers Make

The following are some of the common problems that newbie affiliate marketers make, and these mistakes can cost them their affiliate marketing career.

Trying to make Money without Being Ready to Work

One of the commonest problems with newbie affiliate marketers is trying to make a quick buck, and it never works out. It is hard for a newbie to make money right away because they don't have any content, they have no affiliate marketing knowledge, and no one trusts them. Thus, it is important that you first concentrate on building your content, and once you have a steady stream of traffic, then you can start serving out your affiliate offers.

Not Collecting Emails

As an affiliate marketer, you must remember one thing "the money is in the list"! Thus, your number one mission is to get the email addresses of your leads. Once you have their email addresses, you are free to market the products to them. Some affiliate marketers make the mistake of not gathering their leads' email addresses, and this puts them in a worse situation.

Choosing a Niche they know nothing about

If you look at most successful affiliate marketers, you will realize that they are promoting programs and products that they are passionate about. It is important that you select a niche that you are passionate about. If you are not passionate about a niche, it will show, because you will be less likely to create and market content. But if you are passionate, you will be self-driven, and you will scale the heights of success. Publishing very low-quality content You have to recognize that affiliate marketing, thanks to the nonexistent barriers, attracts all kinds of desperate people – desperate for making money, and the first thing such people do is to publish low-quality blogs and laden the blog post with affiliate links. Of course, the search engines reject such content, and this means the affiliate marketer earns nothing. Thus, it is important that an affiliate marketer focuses on creating powerful and evergreen content so that they might be able to run a profitable business.

Not using Products they recommend

As an affiliate marketer, your work is to create honest reviews about various products so that your audience might try them out as well. Thus, it is incredibly important that you try out a product before you recommend it to other people. If you have not tried a product and you recommend it anyway, and then your audience ends up buying and subsequently finds out that it is a scam, you have betrayed their trust. A significant chunk might opt out of your mail list and choose to do business with someone else.

Relying Solely on Google Traffic

It's true that Google is the grand-daddy of internet traffic. But then you have to diversify your traffic sources if you want to increase your campaign profits. Ensure that you are working with alternative traffic sources, particularly traffic networks, and this should help you run winning marketing campaigns.

Spamming

Desperate affiliate marketers who are probably starving might think that flooding their target audiences with unwanted marketing messages is the way to go. Of course, this approach always fails, and it might put them at risk of account termination from the other end. If you have a tendency of sending out spam, just stop it, else it's going to get you in trouble.

Not Valuing Customers

As an affiliate marketer, always ensure that you hold your customers in high esteem. At the end of the day, they are the ones that support your business. One of the common ways that affiliate marketers fail to respect their customers is by ignoring their requests. Ensure that you answer your customer concerns at all times. This is what gets them excited about working with you. The nicer you become to your customers, the more loyal they become, but if you treat them like trash, you leave them no option but to desert you.

Writing Irrelevant Content

As an affiliate marketer, you must always write relevant content, for this is what attracts your target audience and causes them to take action. If you have a tendency to write irrelevant content, it means that you will attract the wrong crowd, and this will greatly inconvenience your earning capacity. If you don't possess great writing skills, ensure that you work with people who possess great writing skills, and you will soon create awesome content.

Jumping into every Affiliate Program

Affiliate marketers also have the problem of jumping around, joining affiliate programs, and quitting just as quickly. Ensure that you are always measured in your approach with affiliate marketing programs that you join. Ensure that you don't come off as unhinged. Just engage in thorough research beforehand and then select one program. And then focus on promoting the offers. Being focused, you will be in a position to transform your life.

Not Mastering Customer Psychology

If you want to increase your affiliate marketing profits, you absolutely have to put yourself in the shoes of your customers. You have to think like them. But so many affiliate marketers have a very robotic way of doing things. They seem to want to promote products in a very rigid manner, and this stops them from appealing to their target audience. Thus, ensure that you always master your customer psychology so that you may be able to generate great sales.

Not Researching

Some affiliate marketers also don't engage in research, and this causes them to suffer significant losses. When you are researching your content, it helps you stand out, and more customers will want to do business with you. But when you are not engaging in any research, you are likely to come up with low-quality content, and people will give it a wide berth. Always ensure that you research your content.

Scamming

A scammer is the equivalent of an online gangster. They are pretty ruthless. Some affiliate marketers take advantage of the anonymity of the internet and scam people. If you are into that type of behavior, best be assured that your days are numbered. Eventually, your cover will get blown, and people will know you for what you are. Ensure that you are always conducting honest business. As long as you are running an honest business, people will come to you, and you have the potential to make tons of profits. But if you start to scam people, you will only end up with regrets.

Promoting the wrong Product

As an affiliate marketer, you need to have the capacity to understand the connection between what you are promoting and the content that you have already created. For instance, if you operate a blog in the health niche, it is important that you stick to promoting health products, primarily because the readers that your blog attracts are focused on improving their health. Ensure that you promote the right product at all times, and you will see an increase in your campaign profits. If you are promoting the wrong thing, you will undermine your earning potential.

Copying and Pasting

As an affiliate marketer, when you develop the tendency of copying and pasting other people's ad copy, you come across as extremely low IQ. If you have the common sense to understand what a product or service is all about, you certainly can manage to create a powerful marketing message that will stir your target audience and get them to convert into customers.

The Various Forms of Affiliate Marketing Fraud

As an affiliate marketer, you have to be aware of the huge problem that is affiliate fraud. In order to last long and create a great business, you must be willing to stay away from the fraud of any kind. Marketers who fraud other people usually have a bad ending, and they are unable to create a great business. The following are some of the affiliate frauds that you should stay away from:

Click Farms

You may sign up for an affiliate program to promote a product and get paid per valid clicks you send. But then instead of sending valid, you buy clicks from a click farm. This is usually where low paid workers are paid peanuts to spend an entire day clicking on ads. By sending traffic from click farms, you are frustrating the business of your merchant and killing the industry in your own way. But thank goodness there's a powerful technology to detect click farms, and once you are caught engaging in such fraud, you are summarily kicked out without any compensation.

Spamming

As an affiliate marketer, you should go about your business without bothering everyone. But then there are affiliate marketers who assume everyone should get in on the action and they start sending out spam. This can be very annoying on the part of the targeted person. Some people might even go ahead to report your affiliate ID, which could very well put your account on the line.

Ad Stacking

On your website, you are supposed to put one ad on an ad spot. If you put more than one, it means the impressions will count even though the target users will not see the intended ads. This causes the merchant to lose money. Again, it is unwise to engage in such fraud because most affiliate networks have the technology to determine when you are ad stacking.

Stealing Credit Card Details (Formjacking)

As an affiliate marketer, you may have a portal where you require people to submit their credit cards. However, some fraudster affiliate marketers might decide to steal credit card information and use it illegally. Stolen credit cards are a huge "dark" internet business, but it leaves the victims distraught. Stay away from defrauding your target audience so that you may be able to build a powerful business.

See: How to Protect Your Online Business from Formjacking at
https://www.buzzingpoint.com/2020/04/how-to-protect-your-online-business-from-formjacking.html

Conclusion

Affiliate marketing is simply about signing up to become a marketing partner for a merchant or an affiliate network. A merchant is the creator of the product or service, while an affiliate network is usually contracted by many merchants in order to pool together various programs and get affiliate marketers to promote them. Newbie affiliate marketers ought to stick with affiliate networks because the networks provide many programs and a structure that makes it easy to access their funds. The established affiliate marketers may work directly with merchants because they have a great understanding of the market. In as much as affiliate marketing could very well help you attain financial and personal freedom, it doesn't mean that achieving success as an affiliate marketer is akin to snapping your finger. It requires hard work, patience, dedication and access to the right guide.

Other Books by the Author

1. The Passionate Entrepreneur's Strategies: Learn how to discover business ideas that will be successful, grow multiple online income streams, make money from home, attract new & retain customers, applications of SWOT analysis in any business, skills that will help you succeed as an entrepreneur, self-discipline, etc.

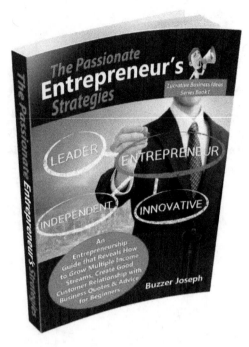

Click to see more about the book: https://www.amazon.com/dp/B089YV65TM

2. How to Make Money Self-Publishing Books for Beginners: Step by Step Guide to Self Publishing a Best Selling Book on Amazon KDP, Design Book Covers with Adobe Photoshop & Promote your Book

OTHER FREE HELPFUL RESOURCES

5 Best Digital Marketing Types and Tips You Should Know - https://www.buzzingpoint.com/2019/07/best-digital-marketing-types-tips.html

20 Best Udemy Online Courses for Personal Development - https://www.buzzingpoint.com/2019/06/best-udemy-online-courses.html

125 Inspiring Business Quotes & Advice from Successful Entrepreneurs - https://www.buzzingpoint.com/2020/04/business-advice-for-entrepreneurs.html

5 Best High in Demand Programming Languages to Learn - https://www.buzzingpoint.com/2019/07/best-programming-languages.html

12 Best Ways to Raise Funds & Save Money for Young Businesses - https://www.buzzingpoint.com/2020/03/ways-save-money-young-business.html

30 Best Worldwide Small Business Grants and How to Secure Them - https://www.buzzingpoint.com/2020/04/best-worldwide-small-business-grants.html

25 Best Lucrative Online and Offline Business Ideas for Students - https://www.buzzingpoint.com/2019/11/lucrative-students-business-ideas.html

5 Best Lucrative Skills You Can Learn Online for Free - https://www.buzzingpoint.com/2019/07/best-online-free-lucrative-skills.html

7 Steps to Help you Start DropShipping Business Online Successfully - https://www.buzzingpoint.com/2020/04/how-to-start-dropshipping-business.html

Tips to Help You Choose the Best Antivirus Software for Your PC - https://www.buzzingpoint.com/2020/04/how-to-choose-best-antivirus-software.html

15 Best Websites You Can Learn Online Skills for Free - https://www.buzzingpoint.com/2019/07/best-websites-learn-skills-free.html

125 Inspiring Business Quotes & Advice from Successful Entrepreneurs - https://www.buzzingpoint.com/2020/04/business-advice-for-entrepreneurs.html

6 Legitimate Simple Ways to Make Money Online for Free - https://www.microsofttut.com/2017/12/6-legitimate-simple-ways-to-make-money-online-free.html

www.ingramcontent.com/pod-product-compliance
Lightning Source LLC
LaVergne TN
LVHW081701050326

832903LV00026B/1861